A·C·S·I
BIBLE

Brendan

Denver, Broncos Rock!!!

GRADE FIVE

Acknowledgements

The Purposeful Design Elementary Bible Series is the product of a remarkable team of Christian educators.

Editorial Team

Dr. Sharon Berry—Managing Editor
Mrs. Mary Jo Kynerd, Miss Renee Pate,
and Dr. Bette Tally—Assistant Editors

Author Team

Mrs. Barbara Alexander, Mrs. Linda Causey,
Mrs. Jan Gillette, Mrs. Laure Herlinger,
Mrs. Marilyn Phillips, Miss Cheri Schoenrock,
Mrs. Darlene Troxel, and Mrs. Connie Williams

purposeful design publications
A Division of ACSI

To enable Christian educators and schools worldwide to effectively prepare students for life

Copyright 1995 by ACSI/Purposeful Design Publications
Reprinted 2001, 2005, 2006

All Rights Reserved. No portion of this book may be reproduced in any form without prior written permission of ACSI/Purposeful Design Publications.

Purposeful Design Publications is the publishing division of the Association of Christian Schools International. ACSI is committed to the ministry of Christian school education, to enable Christian educators and schools worldwide to effectively prepare students for life. As the publisher of books, textbooks, and other educational resources within ACSI, Purposeful Design Publications strives to produce biblically sound materials that reflect Christian scholarship and stewardship, and address the identified needs of Christian schools around the world.

For additional information, write ACSI/Purposeful Design Publications, PO Box 65130, Colorado Springs, CO 80962-5130.
Printed in the United States of America

Scripture quotations are taken from the Holy Bible, New King James Version. Copyright 1982 by Thomas Nelson, Inc. Used by permission. All rights reserved.

ACSI Elementary Bible—Grade Five
ISBN 1-58331-112-2 Student Edition **Catalog** # 7122
ISBN 1-58331-113-0 Teacher Edition **Catalog** # 7123

Purposeful Design Publications
A Division of ACSI
PO Box 65130 • Colorado Springs, CO • 80962-5130

Order Department: 800/367-0798 • Website: http://www.acsi.org

Table of Contents

Page		
5	**Lesson 1**	God's Special Revelation
9	**Lesson 2**	First Things First
13	**Lesson 3**	Abraham: Trust
17	**Lesson 4**	Abraham and Isaac: Obedience
21	**Lesson 5**	Joseph: Rejection and Forgiveness
25	**Lesson 6**	Joseph: Handling False Accusations
29	**Lesson 7**	Moses: Fearing God, Not Man
33	**Lesson 8**	Moses: Choosing God's People
37	**Lesson 9**	Moses: Handling Inadequacies
41	**Lesson 10**	Joshua and Caleb: Standing Alone
45	**Lesson 11**	Joshua: The Leader
49	**Lesson 12**	Achan: Hiding Sin
53	**Lesson 13**	Overview of Judges: Cycle of Sin
57	**Lesson 14**	Deborah: A Helper to Others
61	**Lesson 15**	Gideon: A Man Who Faced Fear
65	**Lesson 16**	Jephthah: Overcoming a Poor Background
69	**Lesson 17**	Samson: Wrong Choices
73	**Lesson 18**	Ruth, Naomi and Boaz: Love and Loyalty
77	**Lesson 19**	Overview of the United Kingdom
81	**Lesson 20**	Samuel: Sensitivity to God
85	**Lesson 21**	Saul: Pride and Disobedience
89	**Lesson 22**	David: Confidence in God
93	**Lesson 23**	David: Sin and Consequences
97	**Lesson 24**	Absalom: Rebellion
101	**Lesson 25**	Solomon: Wisdom
105	**Lesson 26**	Solomon: Talents and Treasures Given to God
109	**Lesson 27**	Overview of the Divided Kingdom
113	**Lesson 28**	Ahab and Elijah: The Fight Between Good and Evil
117	**Lesson 29**	Elisha: Prophet of Miracles and Mercy
121	**Lesson 30**	Isaiah: The Messianic Prophet
125	**Lesson 31**	Jeremiah: God's Weeping Prophet
129	**Lesson 32**	Daniel: Excellent in Spirit
133	**Lesson 33**	Ezra: The Religious Reformer
137	**Lesson 34**	Nehemiah: The Rebuilder
141	**Lesson 35**	Jesus Christ in the Old Testament
145	**Lesson 36**	Overview of the Old Testament
149	**Reference Section**	

God's Special Revelation

1

A

Pack Your Bags — We're Headed Back! Hi, fifth grader! My name is Dr. Diggit and these are my friends, Katie and Austin. Together we're going to investigate some of the most exciting stories and fascinating characters ever. But we can't do it from here; we need to go back. Way back! Back to a time that really existed, a time that really happened. We'll start when only God was moving and making choices, the first choices. He made amazing and loving choices for the world . . . and for us. Now, are you ready?

As we begin our journey, our first job is to help these Bible characters claim their luggage and be on their way. Using the clues on the luggage draw a line from each character to his or her baggage.

5

B **Man's Questions?** Through the ages, people everywhere have asked questions about God. Read 1 Timothy 1:17 and write the verse on the lines. Underline the words that might answer some of the questions people have about God.

> Now to the King eternal, immortal, invisible, to God who alone is wise, be honor and glory forever and ever. Amen.
> 1 Timothy 1:17

Wait a minute, Katie. If God is invisible and we can't see Him, how can we really *know Him?*

Good question, Austin. And it looks like Dr. Diggit already has the answer.

God has chosen to reveal truth about Himself to us through two kinds of revelation.

C **God's Answers!** Find the ways God chose to reveal Himself to man through both general and special revelation. Dr. Diggit has recorded one for you.

History or Governments
Daniel 4:32b

Romans 1:19-20

GENERAL REVELATION

SPECIAL REVELATION

GOD

John 14:6-7

2 Peter 1:20-21

First Things First   2

A Good Beginnings.
Illustrate the events of Creation from Genesis 1.

- **Day 1:** Day, night
- **Day 2:** Sky
- **Day 3:** Grass, plants
- **Day 4:** Stars
- **Day 5:** animals, fish, birds
- **Day 6:** human
- **Day 7:** God rested

Who created the world? **God**

B Unhappy Endings!
Read Genesis 3:1-13 and fill in the word that ends each sentence. Then fill in the "first things" found in this passage.

One day Eve had a conversation with the **serpent**. (v. 1) The serpent was **satan**. (v. 1) The serpent caused the woman to doubt what God said, and Eve was **punished**. (v. 13) When Eve saw that the Tree of the Knowledge of Good and Evil was good for food and would make one wise, she and Adam **sinned**. (v. 6) Adam and Eve knew immediately that they had sinned against God. They sewed fig leaves together to make **coverings**. (v. 7) When they heard God coming to fellowship with them, they were ashamed and crouched behind trees to **hide**. (v. 8) God punished the serpent by causing him to crawl on his belly the rest of his life and eat **dirt**. (v. 14) God punished Adam by allowing thorns and thistles to grow so that all the days of his life man would have to **sin**. (vs. 17-19) Adam and Eve would not live forever but would **die** and return to **dust**. (v. 19)

First — Genesis 3:15
First — Genesis 3:21

C **Charting the Characters.** Investigate what the Bible says about Cain and Abel. Compare the two characters on the chart below. Remember to read all the verses.

Categories	Cain	Abel
Family Background *(Genesis 4:1-2)*	worked the soil	kept flocks
Occupation *(Genesis 4:2)*		
Habits of Worship (Sacrifices) *(Genesis 4:3-4;)* *(Hebrews 11:4)*		
Character Qualities (Actions) *(Genesis 4:5-9)*		
Response to God *(Hebrews 11:4)*		

Go back and check the categories where Cain and Abel made choices.

D **Sketching the Character.** Complete the character sketch of Cain.

Cain was the first son of Adam and _____

_____

_____

_____

E **Questions???** Why didn't God accept Cain's offering? How did Cain's response to God affect his relationship with Him? What was the result of Cain's anger? Who was Cain's wife?

10

2

Jealousy Exposed

Have you ever been afraid of losing a friend or something you loved to somebody else? Or have you ever wanted something someone else had — a CD player or nice clothes or a new bike? How did it make you feel? Jealous . . . or perhaps envious? Remember Cain? He had similar feelings about his brother Abel. Cain could have chosen to love his brother and ask God's forgiveness. Instead, he let his feelings of jealousy grow until he was so angry that he murdered his brother. Some of the Jews in Jesus' day were like Cain. Let's find out how.

F

Jealous Jews. Answer both questions in each passage below. WHY were the Jewish people envious? WHAT actions followed their jealousy?

1. WHY? (*Acts 17:4-6*) _____

   WHAT? _____

2. WHY? (*Acts 13:44-45, 50*) _____

   WHAT? _____
   _____

G

Another Question. What made these Jewish leaders so angry that they wished to bring harm to others?

_____

H

The Jealousy Cure. Read 1 Corinthians 13:4-13 to discover a cure for jealousy and envy.

1. The cure for jealousy and envy is _____.

2. You must give wise advice to someone who has a problem with jealousy or envy. Think of at least three steps he or she can apply to help with the problem. (Clue: Remember what Cain didn't do).

   Step A. _____

   Step B. _____

   Step C. _____

I **Satan's Origin, Fall and Eternal Doom.** Have you ever wondered about God's enemy, Satan? Why did God create him? How much does he affect us? Why doesn't God destroy him if he is so bad? Through the years many people have asked the same questions. The Bible gives us the answers to these questions and also tells us how to defend ourselves against God's enemy, Satan. Remember, Satan is your worst enemy too! Find some answers to these questions by reading the verses and filling in the blanks.

"In Ezekiel 28:12-19 I read that God created Satan and made him _____ (v. 15), but Satan became proud of his _____." (v. 17)

"Wow, the nerve! In Isaiah 14:12-14 Satan made five 'I will' statements that show how he chose to sin by _____." (v. 14)

"What a relief! In Revelation 20:10 God says that Satan will be cast into the _____ _____ and will be tormented _____."

J **Put On Your Armor and Stand.** Read Ephesians 6:10-18. Label the pieces of armor God's soldier should wear to do battle with God's enemy, Satan.

"And I will _____!" (v. 18)

K **Using Your Armor.** Describe one way you might use the Armor of God in a battle against your enemy, Satan. _____

12

Abraham: Trust

A

Abraham's Background. Abraham was a very important man. The Bible tells us that he was called "the friend of God." (James 2:23) Abraham lived in the thriving city of Ur about 2100 B.C. Ur was a **pagan** culture located in the Mesopotamian region close to the Euphrates River. The primary religion was the worship of the moon-god, Nanna. No doubt Abraham's father, Terah, worshiped the moon deity. Perhaps Abraham also worshiped this idol before he met God. But God had other plans for Abraham. We learn about those plans in the very special **covenant** God made with Abraham. Find the words **pagan** and **covenant** in the glossary and finish the definitions on the lines.

1. A **pagan** is _one who is not a christian_.
2. A **covenant** is _an agreement between two people_

B

The Abrahamic Covenant. God promised Abraham three things if he would leave his homeland. Read Genesis 12:2 and list the three promises on the bags below.

- the great name
- blessing to others
- a great nation

C

Dear Diary. Suppose you were Abraham, and God had just asked you to leave your country, friends, home and relatives to go to a strange country. How would you feel? Fearful, sad, excited, or perhaps angry? What would you do? Pretend you are Abraham writing in your diary. Write what he must have thought and what he did based on Genesis 12:4-8.

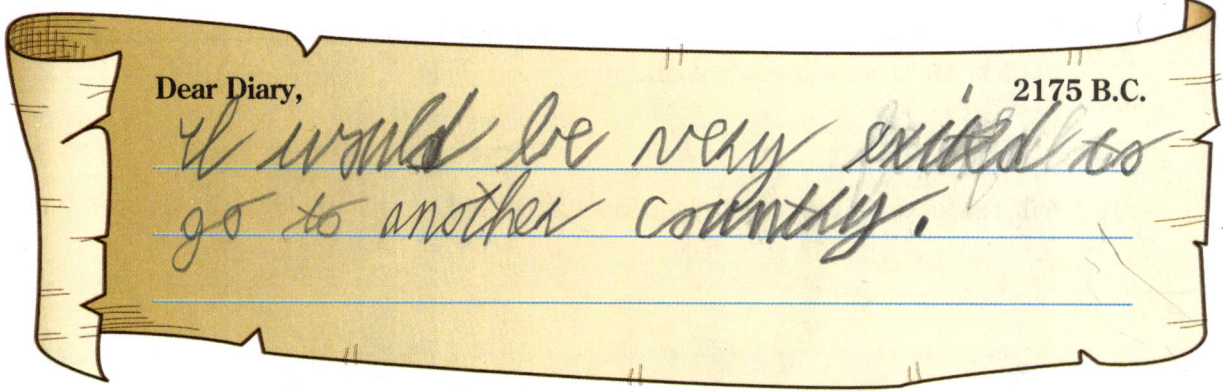

Dear Diary,   2175 B.C.

I would be very excited to go to another country.

D **Family Feud.** A quarrel took place between the herdsmen of Abraham and Lot. What was it about? Who solved the problem? Read Genesis 13 and fill in what might have been said.

The Quarrel (vs. 5-7)
- "I want this land."
- "No, I want this land."

Abram's Solution (vs. 8-9)
- "If you choose right, I'll go left, or right. Go left."

Lot's Choice (vs. 10-13)
- "I choose to go to Sodom."

Abram's Faith (vs. 14-18)
- "This land doesn't look good but you will make it look perfect."

E **Who Really Made the First Choice?** Answer the questions.

1. What characteristic of Abraham helped him feel at peace about letting Lot make the first choice?
   Abram trusted God

2. What characteristic of Lot made him eager to choose the best land first? (A Clue: Lot chose to live in Sodom).
   Selfish

3. What about you? If you had had the same choice as Lot, what would you have done? Why?
   I would have listened to God because im a christian.

14

F

An Everyday Parable. Read the story and answer the questions.

"Someday I'm going to be rich!" thought a young boy. "I don't ever want to worry about money the way my parents do."

The boy became a hard worker. By the time he was a man, he had many skills and a good job. "I'm going to get an even better job to get more money," he thought. And he did.

He bought fine clothes, a fancy car, and a big beautiful home. He put extra money in the bank to keep it safe. "I am rich!" he said. "I have everything I need for the rest of my life." Money became even more important to him than God.

Then one day the rich man died unexpectedly before he had time to become an old man. He had to leave all his money because there is no need for it after death. The man had spent his life earning money and had spent no time preparing for Heaven.

1. Is it wrong to work hard, make a lot of money, save money in the bank, have nice clothes, and buy a nice car or big home? Only if _____

2. Underline the sentence in the story that shows why the man was caught in the trap of greed and wanting things.

3. If the rich man could come back and tell you one thing, what might it be? _____

G

A Bible Parable. Read the parable of the rich man in Luke 12:13-21 to find the answer to these questions.

What choices can I make so I won't want material things more than Godly things?

1. What sin does God warn against? _____

2. What are some things you can do to not put material things before God?

_____

_____

A True Song Story. Have you ever wanted to write the music to a song? Perhaps you have tried pecking out new melodies on the piano or playing a new tune with your recorder, and . . . well, it just wouldn't come out right.

Gospel singer George Beverly Shea once wrote the music to a song in less than one day. Mr. Shea composed "I'd Rather Have Jesus" when he was just twenty years old. One Sunday morning he happened to notice a poem written by Mrs. Rhea F. Miller that his mother had left on the piano. George wrote the music to Mrs. Miller's verse and used the new song a few hours later in the church where his father was pastor.

Mr. Shea has sung, "I'd Rather Have Jesus" more than any other song in his lifetime as a singer; and God has used the words and music to encourage people all over the world to follow His Son, the Lord Jesus Christ.

"I'd Rather Have Jesus" mentions things in the world that would keep us from following God as we should. Read the words to the song and circle the things that sometimes keep you from following God.

I'd Rather Have Jesus

Mrs. Rhea F. Miller
Author

George Beverly Shea
Composer

Verse 1:
I'd rather have Jesus than silver or gold,
I'd rather be His than have riches untold;
I'd rather have Jesus than houses or land,
I'd rather be led by His nail-pierced hand;

Verse 2:
I'd rather have Jesus than men's applause,
I'd rather be faithful to His dear cause;
I'd rather have Jesus than worldwide fame.
I'd rather be true to His holy name:

Verse 3:
He's fairer than lilies of rarest bloom,
He's sweeter than honey from out the comb;
He's all that my hungering spirit needs -
I'd rather have Jesus and let Him lead:

Chorus:
Than to be the king of a vast domain
Or be held in sin's dread sway!
I'd rather have Jesus than anything
This world affords today.

Used by permission, Word Incorporated.

Abraham and Isaac: Obedience

A

Adding Up God's Promises. Dr. Diggit is trying to figure out how many times God renewed His promises to Abraham. Read the verses and check the categories when God repeated the promise.

Scripture	Land	Nation/Seed
1. Genesis 12:1-3	☐	☐
2. Genesis 12:7	☐	☐
3. Genesis 13:14-17	☐	☐
4. Genesis 15:4-7	☐	☐
5. Genesis 17:1-8	☐	☐
6. Genesis 18:10, 18	☐	☐
Total Number		

Remember! When God repeats things in Scripture, He means for us to pay extra attention.

Can you imagine what it would be like to live in a tent — to live in an unprotected environment where wild animals roam and bandits are free to rob? Well, that's exactly what Abraham chose to do. God called him out from the protection of the walled city of Ur to be a tent dweller the rest of his life. Life was certainly not easy, but God was with Abraham confirming His promises.

B

Abraham's False Alarms. Twice Abraham was mistaken about who would fulfill God's promise of a "seed" (son). Find the false alarms.

1. False Alarm #1: Abraham thought _____ might be his promised "seed." (Genesis 15:2-3)

But what did God say? (Genesis 15:4) Yes. _____ No. _____

2. False Alarm #2: Abraham thought _____ might be his promised "seed." (Genesis 17:18)

But what did God say? (Genesis 17:19) Yes. _____ No. _____

C

The Real Promised Son. Read Genesis 21:1-3 and write their names.

Mother: _____

Father: _____

Son: _____

If Abraham was 75 years old when God promised to send a son and 25 years went by, how old was Abraham when Isaac was born?

_____

D **Missing Facts.** If Abraham, and his son Isaac, had lived in today's world, their story on Mt. Moriah would have been a best seller. Help Dusty check out these incredible events. Read Genesis 22. Using the references in Dr. Diggit's diary, fill in the missing facts.

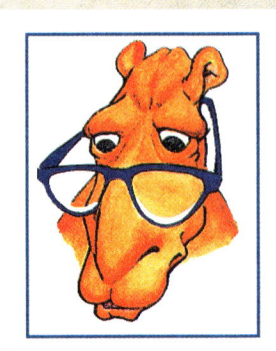

WHO?
Father _____ and his only son, _____ (v. 2)

WHAT?
God said, "Take your only son, Isaac, and _____ him as a _____." (v. 2)

WHEN?
Abraham went _____ in the _____ On the _____ day he came to the place. (vs. 3-4)

HOW?
Abraham took the _____ to _____ his _____. (v. 10)

WHERE?
God said, "Go to _____ to one of the _____ of which I shall tell you." (v. 2)

WHY?
Because God was _____ His servant Abraham. (v. 10)

E **Abraham's Response.** Describe the attitude with which Abraham obeyed God.

_____

_____

F **Reading Old Testament Pictures.** How is the story of Abraham and Isaac a picture of God the Father and His Son? _____

_____

4

G On the Road to Obedience.

On the Road to Obedience — Game Board

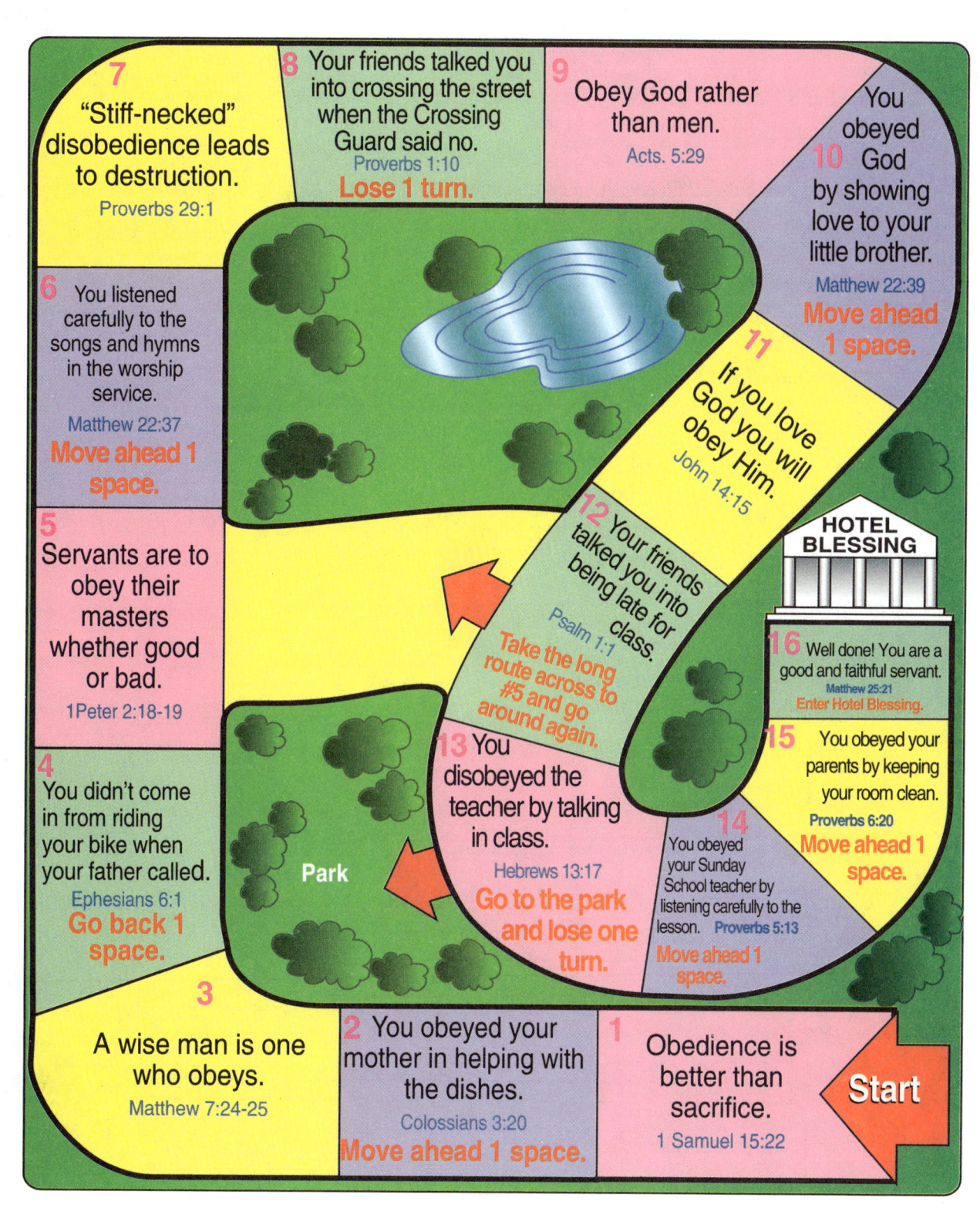

Start →

1. Obedience is better than sacrifice. 1 Samuel 15:22

2. You obeyed your mother in helping with the dishes. Colossians 3:20 *Move ahead 1 space.*

3. A wise man is one who obeys. Matthew 7:24-25

4. You didn't come in from riding your bike when your father called. Ephesians 6:1 *Go back 1 space.*

5. Servants are to obey their masters whether good or bad. 1 Peter 2:18-19

6. You listened carefully to the songs and hymns in the worship service. Matthew 22:37 *Move ahead 1 space.*

7. "Stiff-necked" disobedience leads to destruction. Proverbs 29:1

8. Your friends talked you into crossing the street when the Crossing Guard said no. Proverbs 1:10 *Lose 1 turn.*

9. Obey God rather than men. Acts 5:29

10. You obeyed God by showing love to your little brother. Matthew 22:39 *Move ahead 1 space.*

11. If you love God you will obey Him. John 14:15

12. Your friends talked you into being late for class. Psalm 1:1 *Take the long route across to #5 and go around again.*

13. You disobeyed the teacher by talking in class. Hebrews 13:17 *Go to the park and lose one turn.*

14. You obeyed your Sunday School teacher by listening carefully to the lesson. Proverbs 5:13 *Move ahead 1 space.*

15. You obeyed your parents by keeping your room clean. Proverbs 6:20 *Move ahead 1 space.*

16. Well done! You are a good and faithful servant. Matthew 25:21 *Enter Hotel Blessing.*

19

Remember how Abraham obeyed God promptly and completely in every way? He proved his love for God by the choice he made to obey God. Abraham obeyed willingly with his thoughts and heart attitude, and he obeyed immediately with his spoken words and actions. Let's think of Abraham's good example to us as we make our choices to trust and obey the authorities God has placed over us.

H Good and Bad One-Liners.
By evaluating their thoughts and words, decide whether the student responses are good or bad. Check the appropriate column and write a reason for your choice.

	Good	Bad
#1 Mary thought, "I'll do it without complaining." Reason: ___	☑	☐
#2 Jim thought, "I should do math, but I'll draw." Reason: ___	☐	☑
#3 Sally said, "Why can't Sue do it, Mom? I'm busy." Reason: ___	☐	☑
#4 Bill responded, "Sure, Dad, I'll mow the yard now." Reason: ___	☑	☐
#5 Dan thought, "O.K., Mom. I'll DO it! I'll DO it!" Reason: ___	☑	☐
#6 Ned said, "Yes, I'll help at recess, Mrs. Jones." Reason: ___	☑	☐
#7 Liz thought, "Mrs. Jones won't see me write notes." Reason: ___	☐	☐

I Setting Goals.
Think of when it has been hard to obey at home and at school. Set some future goals. Fill in what your authorities might ask of you and how you will respond.

My parents might ask, _____.

I will say, _____.

My teacher might say, _____.

I will say, _____.

20

Joseph: Rejection and Forgiveness

A Family Ties.
How would you like to have brothers like Joseph? They certainly made some bad choices. Even though they were cruel to him, God had a future plan for Joseph and his brothers. Jacob's twelve sons were to have a big part in forming the nation of Israel. So . . . let's find out about Joseph's very important family. Using Genesis 49, circle the names of the twelve sons of Jacob.

X	N	B	P	R	E	U	B	E	N	W	I	P	F	R
N	O	E	M	I	S	J	J	R	X	D	L	C	V	W
S	W	N	B	K	L	U	M	O	N	I	A	E	Y	P
C	F	J	H	U	F	D	V	Y	S	C	T	G	T	M
T	U	A	Q	V	R	A	A	C	G	E	H	A	L	C
W	J	M	C	Y	X	H	S	K	D	E	P	F	K	L
A	Z	I	R	B	N	D	H	V	E	M	A	H	B	E
L	P	N	U	L	U	B	E	Z	R	V	N	A	D	V
A	S	G	L	V	E	T	R	A	H	C	A	S	S	I

B Brotherly Hate.
Read Genesis 37 and describe Joseph's brothers' evil thoughts, words and actions. Fill in the facts.

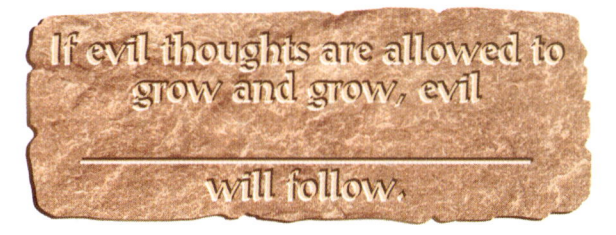

If evil thoughts are allowed to grow and grow, evil _____ will follow.

Their Thoughts. (vs. 3-4) _____

_____

Their Words. (vs. 18-20) _____

_____

Their Actions. (vs. 23-32) _____

_____

Record the brothers' real problem.

_____

Clue: Genesis 37:11

C. A Sad Day for Joseph.
Katie is thinking how Joseph's brothers sold him into slavery. Using Genesis 37, complete her thoughts.

Joseph must have been so sad. He was so young, only __17__ years old. It was so mean of his brothers to take his __coat__. Joseph __loved__ it because his father had given it to him. How sad. Wow! It must have been scary to be thrown into a smelly old __pit__. And I thought my brother was bad! Joseph's brothers sold him for money to be a slave in __Egypt__. Joseph must have felt __bad__. But Joseph responded __pray__.

D. A Glad Day for Joseph.
Read Genesis 50 and answer the questions.

1. What did Joseph's brothers ask of Joseph? (vs. 17-18)
   __to forgive__

2. What does verse 18 show us about Joseph's first dreams about his brothers?
   __his dream came true__

3. What was Joseph's attitude when he forgave his brothers? (vs. 19-21)
   __nice__

E. Find Joseph's Secret.
Cross out two letters and leave the third letter blank on both lines below. The blank letters will tell what Joseph believed about God that helped him forgive his brothers.

XYHKLEFFBLKEIYL0PIAQECVVJHELMDPJIRFNWSGUJO
WSDPLSQASLPOEDVWSEWSRVCEHBIWSGNMNNJTHGY

5

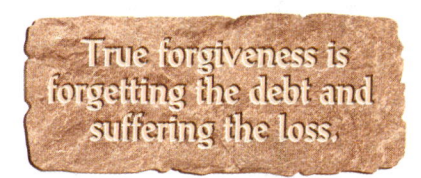

True forgiveness is forgetting the debt and suffering the loss.

Learning How to Truly Forgive. True forgiveness is tough! We can say all the right words: "I'm sorry," or "I apologize," or "Please forgive me," yet we still do not forgive as God desires us to do. To please God when we forgive, we must get rid of those "U O Me's."

F

Check Out the Letters. Jason and Mark had a problem at recess yesterday. Jason has written two letters asking forgiveness for his part in the problem. Check the box on the letter which shows that Jason has gotten rid of his "U O Me's". Give a reason for your choice below.

> Dear Mark,
>
> I'm sorry that I hurt you yesterday by making ugly comments about your new braces. I know I was wrong. Will you forgive me? From now on I'm going to try real hard to choose words that will encourage instead of hurt. Will you pray for me?
>
> Your friend,
> Jason

> Dear Mark,
>
> I'm sorry that I hurt you yesterday by making ugly comments about your new braces. Will you forgive me? I know I was wrong, but I only said that because you made fun of my glasses. I think you owe me an apology, too.
>
> Your friend,
> Jason

Write the reason for your choice. _____

G

Getting Rid of the "U O Me's." Use the clues to answer the questions.

Clue #1
We must first believe some things.

Clue #2
We must choose to do some things.

What must we believe? (Romans 8:28)
_____

What must we choose to do? (Colossians 3:13)
_____

How can believing Romans 8:28 help us forgive others and get rid of those "U O Me's"?
_____
_____

Sharing God's Forgiveness. Sharing God's forgiveness through a tract can make a big difference in a person's life. You need to remember, though, that it's not just a picture or the writing on the tract that makes the difference. It's the truth of the Word of God! Check the following real life examples.

Numerous children have come to know the Lord Jesus Christ after reading children's tracts.

A 93-year-old Chinese woman in Canton, China, became a Christian after reading a Chinese tract someone had given her.

A small youth group of five young people and one adult leader in London, England, all received Christ after one of the young persons read a tract to the whole group.

H **A Three Point Tract Message.** A good tract that helps people become Christians usually has at least three important truths. Read the references and write the truth in a short statement.

1. Romans 3:23 _____

2. 1 Corinthians 15:3 _____

3. John 3:36 _____

I **"U Make a Tract."** Follow the directions below to make a tract.

a. Fold a piece of white bond paper in half lengthwise.
b. Cut into two pieces at the fold.
c. Fold each of the two pieces in half again. Open up.
d. Print the above three truth statements with references on the inside, centering the words on the page.
e. Design an eye-catching cover and color it.

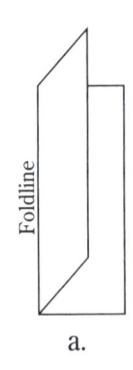

Joseph: Handling False Accusations

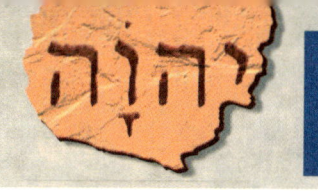

6

A   **A Story of Real Courage.** Read the true story of Jim Elliot below and do the activities that follow.

Jim Elliot — 20th Century Martyr

Have you ever wondered what it would be like to live as a missionary in a hostile jungle surrounded by poisonous snakes and plants? Sound scary? You bet! But Jim Elliot was a 20th century hero who did just that. He was a missionary called by God to take the Gospel into the dangerous territory of the dreaded Auca Indians in Ecuador, South America.

Jim Elliot was born the third son of Fred and Clara Elliot in 1927 in Portland, Oregon. His father was an evangelist. Both parents were staunch Christians who read and taught the Bible to their children daily. Obedience and honesty were the qualities most emphasized in Jim's home. Because Jim learned to obey his parents cheerfully when he was young, he willingly followed God's leading later to serve on the mission field.

From the early age of six, young Jim was confident of his salvation. One night after a church meeting Jim said to his mother, "Now, Mama, the Lord Jesus can come whenever He wants. He could take our whole family, because I'm saved now. . . ." Jim's testimony to others was crystal clear. He carried his Bible to school and told everyone he met about Jesus.

Sometimes friends would put pressure on Jim to do things that were not pleasing to God. Once in high school a popular student, who was a star athlete and student president, tried to persuade him to attend an activity that Jim felt was inappropriate for a Christian. He boldly shared his reason for saying no to the activity. "I'm a Christian and the Bible says that I'm in the world but not of it. That's why I'm not going."

In college Jim believed that God was leading him to the mission field in South America. He was so convinced that fellowship with God was the most important thing in life he even set his alarm extra early so that he could study more of God's Word and pray. In a letter to his younger sister he encouraged her to do the same. He wrote, "Begin each day with private reading of the Word and prayer."

Some years later Jim's dream of becoming a missionary in the jungles of Ecuador, South America, came true. He quickly became a trusted friend of the Quichua Indians as he learned their language and taught them the Bible. It wasn't long before he desired to go to another part of the jungle — a part of the jungle where the white man had feared to go — where the killer Auca Indians lived. When Jim was questioned about going to a killer tribe, he replied, "I am ready to die for the salvation of the Aucas." Jim and four other missionaries made plans to take the Gospel of Christ to the Aucas.

The men landed a small plane on the beach of the Curray River in Auca territory. Three days after their arrival, three Aucas came to the beach. The first contact was surprisingly friendly. Jim gave gifts to the Aucas; one Indian even took a ride in the plane. Jim and his group waited again. Several days later a group of Aucas came to the beach, this time with wooden spears. The missionaries had come prepared with firearms to defend themselves but chose not to use them. The Aucas killed all five missionaries and destroyed their plane.

Several years before Jim Elliot was martyred, he wrote, "God, I pray Thee, light these idle sticks of my life and may I burn for Thee. Consume my life, my God, for it is Thine. I seek not a long life, but a full one, like You, Lord Jesus."

1. Circle two character qualities that helped Jim follow God.

2. Put a wavy line under three action phrases that show Jim's testimony.

3. Underline the reason Jim gives for choosing not to go to a certain activity.

4. Put brackets around the phrase that tells what was most important to Jim.

5. Shade the sentence that shows what Jim was willing to do for God.

6. Box the phrase that shows Jim's heart desire.

B **Write a Journal Entry.** Jim Elliot wrote often in his journal about what God was teaching him through the Word. Read 1 Peter 4:12-19 and write a journal entry of your own describing what God is saying to you about suffering for Christ.

My Journal Entry
Date

Moses: Fearing God, Not Man   7

A
The Bondage Breaker. Follow the maze to discover what God required of Israel before they were delivered from bondage. As you come to each reference in Exodus, identify the plague, then answer the question. Before they were delivered, what did God require of Israel? (12:13)

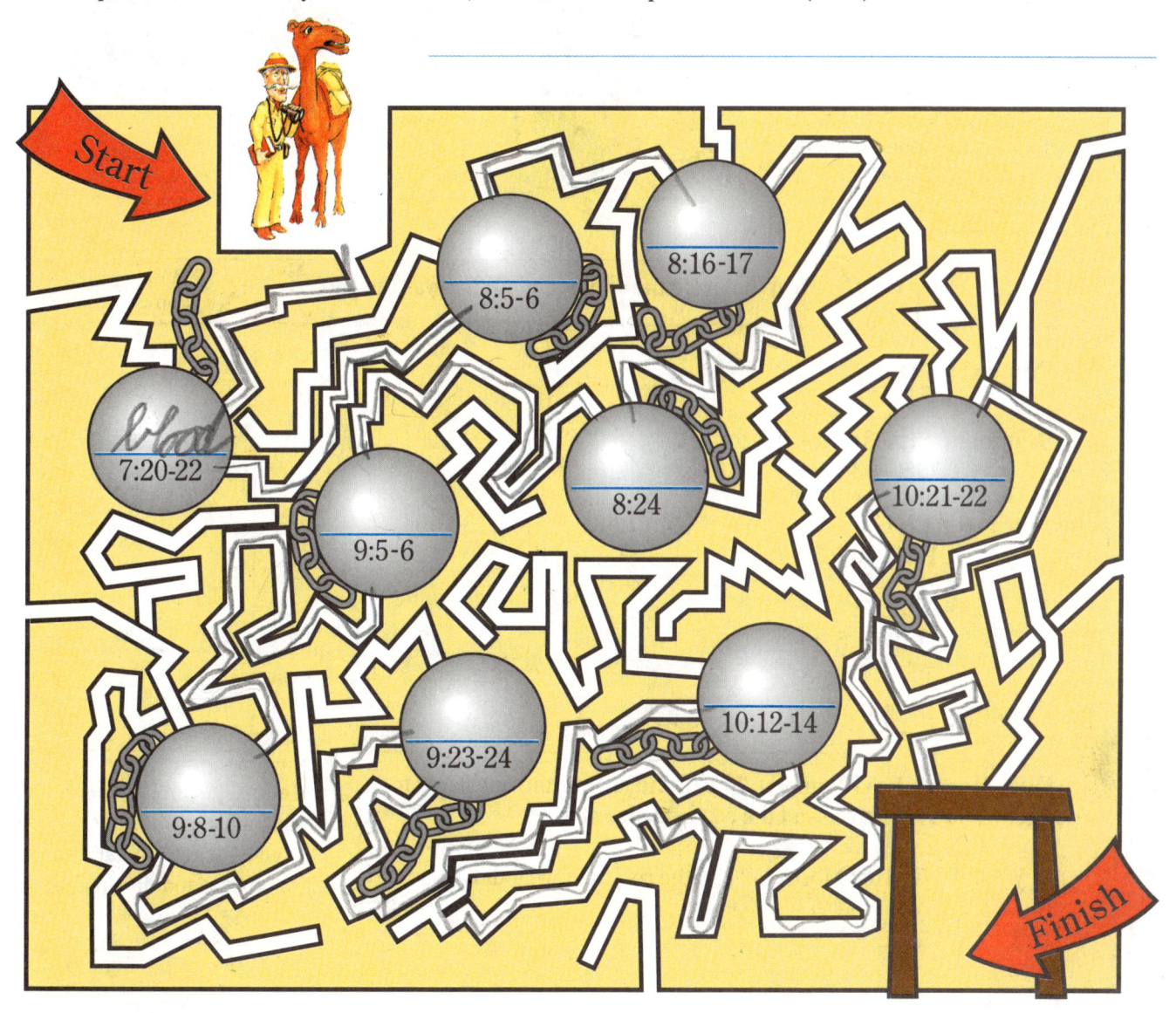

_____

- 7:20-22 — blood
- 8:5-6
- 8:16-17
- 9:5-6
- 8:24
- 10:21-22
- 9:8-10
- 9:23-24
- 10:12-14

Start → Finish

B
Making Connections. Dr. Diggit has made some very important connections. Let's see if you can too! Compare Exodus 12:23 and Hebrews 9:22. Write a description of how the Passover is like Christ's death for our sins.

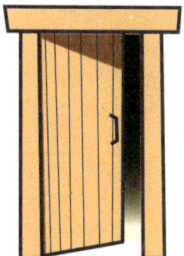

_____
_____
_____
_____

C **Choices and Consequences.** Throughout their journey to the Promised Land, the Children of Israel made some bad choices. Read the verses and record on the chart some of their choices and consequences.

Scripture	Who made the choice?	What was the choice?	What was the consequence?
Numbers 11:1	people	complained	consumed by fire
Numbers 11:4-6; 11:33-34	people	craving meat	great plagues
Numbers 12:1-2; 12:9-10,15	Meriam	they complained bout Moses	Meriam got leprosy
Numbers 16:1-3; 16:31-35	Korah and his company	they rebelled	the earth ate them
Numbers 21:4-6	people	complained to Moses and God	bit by a snake and died

D **Even Moses.** Read Numbers 20:7-12 and answer the questions to discover Moses' choice and the consequence of it.

Hmm . . . even God's servant Moses made a bad choice and suffered a sad consequence. What does it mean? . . . I guess God doesn't play favorites.

1. What did God tell Moses to do to the rock and what did Moses do?

_____
_____

2. What sin did Moses commit and what was the consequence of his sin?

_____

E **Even Me.** Read Hebrews 12:11. What good comes to your life when God chastens you?

_____
_____

F

Get Set! GO! God gave the Children of Israel some commands and some good reasons for obeying those commands. Read the verses in Joshua 1 and complete the "why".

1. ". . . go over this Jordan. . . ." (v. 2) Why? _____
   _____

2. ". . . meditate in it (God's Law) day and night. . . ." (v. 8) Why? _____
   _____

3. "Be strong and of good courage; do not be afraid. . . ." (v. 9) Why?
   _____
   _____

G

Crossing Over. Dr. Diggit and a native tent dweller are exploring to see who crossed over the Jordan River. Read the verses below. Match the verse to the question by drawing a line, then answer the question.

```
G B P B U R O N N M
  G C I U B S C E G
      C C N A G B B C R N N K C B U P O G
                            N W B U E G R N C
```

Joshua 1:16	Who instructed the priests to lead the people?	_____
Joshua 1:18	Who wanted the disobedient ones to die?	_____
Joshua 3:6	Who carried the Ark across the Jordan River?	_____
Joshua 3:17	Who obeyed God by following His chosen leader?	_____

H

Crossing Out. Cross out all the B's, C's, G's, N's, and U's in the river above. Fill in the three things that made Israel know God was with them when they crossed the Jordan.

God's P _____ God's A _____ God's P _____

I **Puzzling Questions.** Perhaps you've wondered about the "fear of the Lord". If God is loving, then why would He tell us to fear Him? Read the verses and fill in a description of what God-fearing people were like, what they did, and how they felt.

(Exodus 1:17) The _____ feared God and they _____ .

(Exodus 14:31) _____ feared the Lord and they _____ .

(Job 1:1) _____ feared God and he was _____ .

(Acts 10:1-2) _____ feared God and he _____ .

(Proverbs 16:6) People who fear the Lord will _____ .

(Proverbs 19:23) People who have the fear of the Lord will be _____ .

The fear of the Lord is the _____

Proverbs 9:10

J **Putting the Puzzle Together.** Now, see if you can write your own definition of "the fear of the Lord". Your answers in Exercise I might help you.

The fear of the Lord is _____

Moses: Choosing God's People 8

A. Birth Certificate.
Dr. Diggit has just returned from an exciting dig! He thinks he might have found Moses' birth certificate, but it's so old the words aren't clear. Read the verses in Exodus and help him fill in family background about Moses.

BIRTH CERTIFICATE OF M o s e s

- Meaning of Baby's Name: _To draw out of water._ (2:10)
- Date of Birth: _1526 B.C._ (Bible Dictionary)
- Place of Birth: _Egypt_ (1:1)
- Tribe: _Levi_ (2:1)
- Race: _Hebrew_ (2:11)
- Father: _Amram_ (6:20)
- Mother: _Jochebed_ (6:20)
- Older Sister: _Miriam_ (15:20)
- Older Brother: _Aaron_ (7:1)
- Adopted Mother: _Pharaoh Daughter_ (2:10)

B. Family Relationships.
Read the verses in Exodus and write how the following people were related to each other. (Careful! The last two are tricky.)

- Moses and Jethro were _son-in-law_ & _father-in-law_. (3:1)
- Zipporah and Moses were _wife_ & _husband_. (18:2)
- Gershom and Eliezer were _brother_ & _brother_. (18:3-4)
- Zipporah and Gershom were _mother_ & _son_. (2:21-22)
- Moses and Eliezer were _father_ & _son_.
- Jethro and Zipporah were _father_ & _daughter_.

C **Charting the Choices.** Austin and Katie drew a flowchart to help see Moses' choices. Read Hebrews 11:24-27. Choose a word from the word bank that fits best and write the number on the appropriate blank.

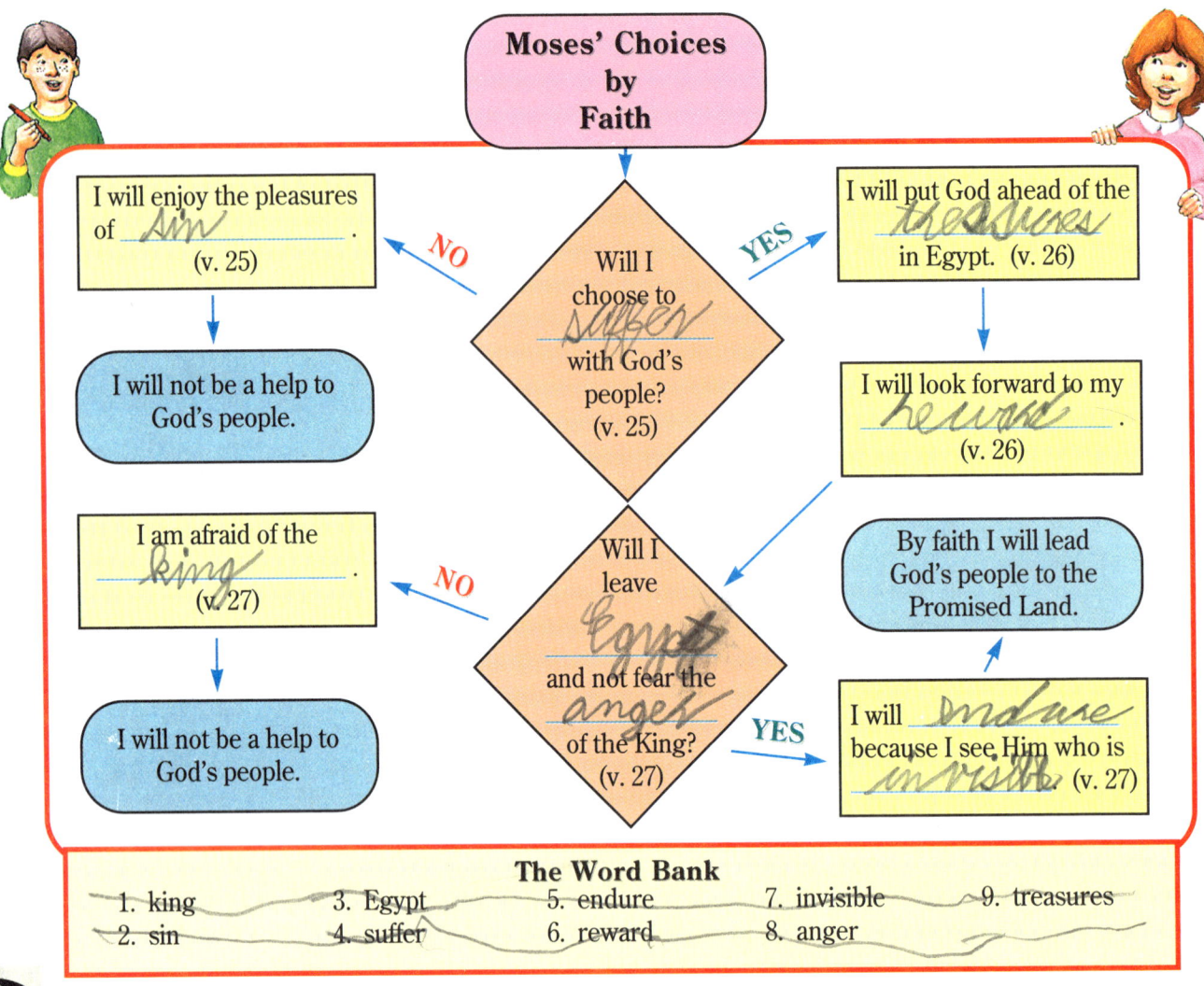

Moses' Choices by Faith

- Will I choose to _suffer_ with God's people? (v. 25)
  - NO → I will enjoy the pleasures of _sin_. (v. 25) → I will not be a help to God's people.
  - YES → I will put God ahead of the _treasures_ in Egypt. (v. 26) → I will look forward to my _reward_. (v. 26)

- Will I leave _Egypt_ and not fear the _anger_ of the King? (v. 27)
  - NO → I am afraid of the _king_. (v. 27) → I will not be a help to God's people.
  - YES → I will _endure_ because I see Him who is _invisible_. (v. 27) → By faith I will lead God's people to the Promised Land.

The Word Bank

1. king
2. sin
3. Egypt
4. suffer
5. endure
6. reward
7. invisible
8. anger
9. treasures

D **Interpreting the Choices.** Answer the questions.

What two choices was Moses willing to make to identify with God's people?

He chose to give up treasures and

What kinds of things was Moses willing to give up to identify with God's people?

He chose to

What reward was Moses looking forward to when he made choices to identify with God's people?

What characteristics about Moses would you most like to have in your life? Why?

E **Moses the Intercessor.** Moses became a great intercessor for God's people! Read one of his intercessory prayers in Numbers 14:11-19 to find out exactly why he interceded for Israel. Circle the letter that best answers each question.

1. Why did Moses ask God to save Israel?
   a. Moses did not want to look like a failure.
   b. Moses felt Israel deserved to be forgiven.
   c. Moses wanted God's reputation to remain good.
   d. Moses wanted to show Israel that he loved God.
   e. Moses didn't want Israel put to death.

2. Who was Moses really concerned about?
   a. himself
   b. Israel
   c. other nations
   d. God

F **Motivation for Intercession.** Examine the four prayers and circle the one that best follows Moses' example.

Dear Lord, forgive Jenny and help her not to tell lies anymore. Because... if she doesn't stop, my mom won't let me go to her house again. In Jesus' name, Amen.

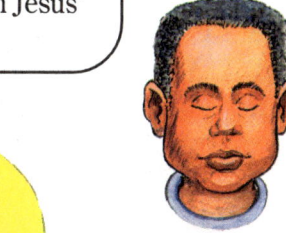

Dear Lord Jesus, please help James to get over the flu. He is very sick, and I really don't think he deserves to be so miserable. He's such a nice guy! In Jesus' name, Amen.

Dear Lord, I am praying for William. Please help him not to blow up all the time. The guys on the soccer team need to see Your power at work so they will know You are real. In Jesus' name, Amen.

Dear Father, please help Nell. I told her I would pray that she would do well on the math test. If she doesn't do well, Nell will think I didn't pray. In Jesus' name, Amen.

Write the reason for your choice. _____
_____
_____

G **The Great Prayer Example.** Study the Lord's Prayer in Matthew 6:9-13. Answer the questions below.

1. Use your glossary to find the meaning of the word "hallowed." What are you doing when you pray that the Lord's name is "hallowed"? _____

2. In what verse does Jesus praise God? What does Jesus say about God? _____

3. What were some of the daily needs Jesus asked God to provide? _____

4. According to verse 12 what should we ask God to do? _____

5. What did Jesus ask in verse 13? _____

H **What's a Prayer Pact?** Unscramble the letters to find how the word PACT can remind us of the way Jesus taught us to pray. Transfer your answers to the outer circle at the right. Use the inner lines for personal examples.

1. **P** _ _ _ _ _ _ _
   (s i g a n i r)

2. **A** _ _ _ _ _
   (k i g s n)

3. **C** _ _ _ _ _ _ _ _ _
   (n f s e o s n i g)

4. **T** _ _ _ _ _ _ _
   (g a h k n i n)

MY PERSONAL PRAYER PACT WITH GOD

36

Moses: Handling Inadequacies   9

A  **Which Attribute?** Dr. Diggit has just made a list of some of God's attributes. Read Exodus 3:7-10. Circle the attribute that you think motivated God to call Moses for the job. Give a reason for your choice. (See your glossary to review the attributes).

Reason: _Because he wanted to test Moses faith._

Read Exodus 3:10. What job did God want Moses to do? _Preach to people in Egypt._

B **"But Lord. . . ."** Read the verses in Exodus and paraphrase God's answers to Moses' concerns.

Moses' "But Lord" Concerns	God's "But Moses" Answers
"But Lord, I'm a nobody. Why would the Pharoah of Egypt listen to me?" (3:11)	I will be with you. (3:12)
"But Lord, if I go to the people of Israel, who will I tell them You are? What is Your name?" (3:13)	I am who I am. (3:14-15)
"But Lord, what if the people won't believe me? What if they say You haven't really sent me?" (4:1)	What is that in your hand? (4:2-9)
"But Lord, I can't talk to people very well. I have never been a good speaker." (4:10)	I will help you speak. (4:11-12)
"But Lord, please send someone else in my place to do the job." (4:13)	What about your brother? (4:14-17)

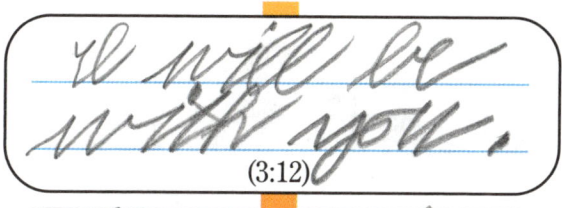

37

C **Who Built the Tabernacle?** Austin and Katie are wondering who helped build the Tabernacle. Read the verses in Exodus and draw a line matching the questions to the person or group.

Israel	Who was appointed chief craftsman? (31:1-5)
gifted artisans	Who was chosen as the assistant craftsman? (31:6-11)
Bezalel	Who taught the craftsmen their skills? (35:30-35)
God	Who gave too many offerings to build the Tabernacle? (36:3-7)
Aholiab	Who else did God choose to do His work? (36:1-2)

D **A Bird's-Eye View.** Below is a diagram of the Tabernacle. Read the verses from Exodus and label the parts of the Tabernacle. (Some have already been done.)

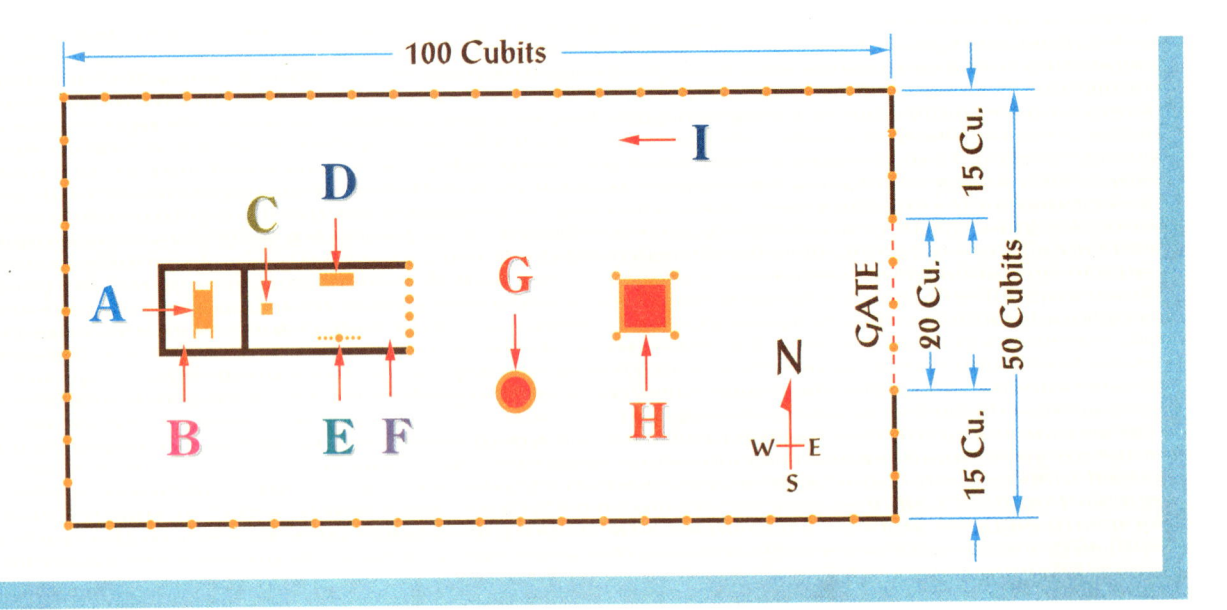

A. _____ (37:1)   B. Holy of Holies

C. _____ _____ (37:25)

D. _____ of Showbread (37:10)   E. _____ (37:17)

F. Holy Place   G. _____ (38:8)

H. _____ of the _____ (38:1)   I. _____ (38:9)

38

E Finding God's Gifts.
Dr. Diggit has been digging again, this time in Romans 12. He has found some of the gifts God has given to Christians. Using the clues, find the gifts to solve the puzzle. Words may be exactly the same or slightly different in your Bible.

Down
1. Speaks out boldly for God. (v. 6)
2. Helps meet the needs of others. (v. 7)
3. Contributes to the needs of others. (v. 8)

Across
4. Makes the Bible clear to others. (v. 7b)
5. Encourages others to serve the Lord. (v. 8)
6. Organizes events in an orderly way. (v. 8)
7. Comforts those who are hurting. (v. 8)

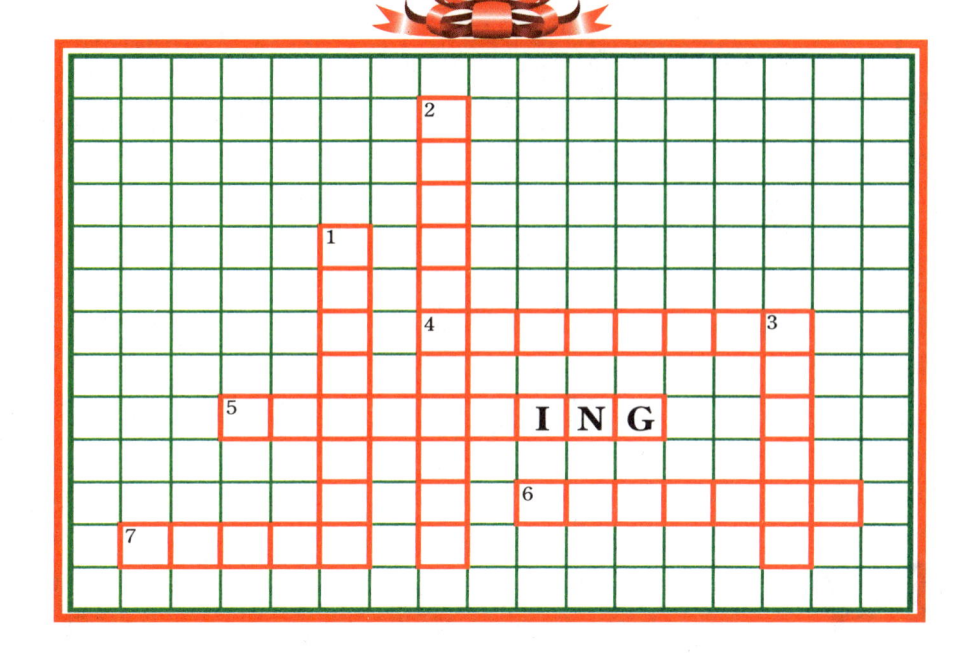

F Seeing Spiritual Gifts.
Many times God's people respond to everyday situations according to the gifts God has given to them. Listen to your teacher read "The Accident." Then read the student responses on the gift boxes. From the above list label the tag with the gift each student might have.

"Here, John, use my handkerchief."

"We can keep this from happening, John. Next time we'll play on the grassy part."

"I feel so bad for you, John."

"Wow, you really needed to be wearing your tennis shoes, John." (Clue: No question about it!)

"Wow! It was that gravel that made you fall, John." (Clue: Reason is clear!)

"Bill, you go get a towel; and Sue, you get the teacher. I'll help John up."

"Hey, John, after school when you're all taped up, I'll treat you to ice cream."

39

G **Day of Atonement.** Read the verses in Leviticus 16 and fill in the missing words.

Once a _____ (v. 34) the high priest went to the most _____ _____ (v. 16) to make _____ (v. 16) for Israel's _____ (v. 30). The high priest took _____ _____ (v. 7) and presented them before the door of the _____ of _____ (v. 7). After casting lots, one goat was named the Lord's, and it was killed for a _____ _____ (v. 9). Its blood was sprinkled over the _____ _____ (v. 15). The other goat was the _____ (v. 10) and was presented alive. The priest laid his _____ (v. 21) on the live goat, confessed Israel's sin and released it into the _____ (v. 22).

H **Break the Code.** Each number below represents a letter of the alphabet. One equals A, two equals B, three equals C and so on for the rest of the alphabet. Use the numbers to write a Bible verse. (Three letters will change to numbers).

"for he made him who
 6 15 18   8 5   13 1 4 5   8 9 13 23 8 15

knew no sin to be
11 14 5 23   14 15   19 9 14   20 15   2 5

sin for us, that we
19 9 14   6 15 18   21 19   20 8 1 20   23 5

might become the
13 9 7 8 20   2 5 3 15 13 5   20 8 5

righteousness of
18 9 7 8 20 5 15 21 19 14 5 19 19   15 6

god in him."
7 15 4   9 14   8 9 13

2 Corinthians 5:21
B   3 15 18 9 14 20 8 9 1 14 19   E U

40

Joshua and Caleb: Standing Alone

A

Seeing Things the Same. Dr. Diggit, Dusty, Austin and Katie are spying out the Scriptures. Read Numbers 13 to answer their questions with a one-word description.

What did all the spies see . . .

in the land? _fruit_
(13:26-27)

in the cities? _____
(13:28)

in the people? _grasshoppers_
(13:33)

Whom did all the spies see?
(See 13:29 and circle the answers in the word find.)

A	A	M	A	L	E	K	I	T	E	S	K	U	S
I	O	E	S	K	E	I	S	S	M	M	T	E	S
S	S	J	E	C	D	K	J	C	I	B	A	H	E
P	S	E	T	I	N	A	A	N	A	C	T	H	B
Q	P	B	I	O	E	V	M	Y	W	M	V	U	G
Z	R	U	T	P	Q	B	N	O	M	C	K	K	G
E	I	S	T	I	N	O	I	E	R	B	P	A	A
P	G	I	I	F	T	Z	H	I	K	I	O	L	H
M	P	T	H	I	J	E	B	U	S	I	T	E	S
Q	O	E	N	K	G	Z	J	U	P	W	F	E	E
S	F	S	S	O	P	E	F	R	O	Z	A	K	S

B

Seeing Things Differently. The spies saw the same things, but they surely didn't respond the same way. Using the verses in Numbers, list their different responses.

Verses	Joshua and Caleb	Other Spies
13:30-33		
14:2-6	explore	give up
14:7-10	want the land	stone them!

Explain the differences in the attitudes of Joshua and Caleb and the other ten spies. (Clue: 13:30-31;14:6-9)

_____
_____

C **A Match for Our "Giants."** Read the verses from the list below. Choose three verses that you think would make good ammunition to fight each of the "giants." Write the reference and a reason for your choice on the lines under each picture. (Ephesians 1:4; Matthew 28:20; Philippians 4:13; 1 John 1:9)

D **Giants of the Faith.** Follow the directions below.

1. What happened to the ten fearful spies? Why? What happened to Joshua and Caleb? Why? (See Numbers 14:36-38.)

2. Write the phrase from Joshua 14:13-14 which shows why God blessed Caleb by giving him Hebron.

3. Think of a time when God blessed you for obeying. Write about it on the lines below.

42

E

Dear Gabby. Pretend you are Gabby, an advice columnist for a local newspaper. "Help Me" has just written to you asking advice about handling peer pressure. Use the truths in Proverbs 1:8-19 to write your answer. (Clue: There are at least four pieces of advice).

> Dear Gabby,
> My friends talk me into things I shouldn't do. What should I do?
> Sincerely,
> Help Me

Dear Help Me,

_____
_____
_____
_____
_____

Your friend,
Gabby

F

What Would You Choose to Do If . . . ? Read the situations below and circle the choice God would want you to make in each.

1. If the most popular student in my class said to me, "Did you know that Jamie made a D on her report card?" I would choose to…
   a. continue asking for more information about it.
   b. tell other friends and then say, "Pray for Jamie."
   c. explain that Jamie always makes bad grades.
   d. say, "I don't think we should talk about it."

2. If during a test my best friend whispered, "What's your answer to number five?" I would choose to. . .
   a. tell the teacher later that day.
   b. shake my head for "No."
   c. only help by giving a clue with finger motions.
   d. give the answer but tell my friend, "No More!"

3. If I was with a group of friends who decided to watch a video my parents did not approve of, I would choose to. . .
   a. watch only a little and then leave.
   b. say, "My parents would not approve," and go home.
   c. watch it and tell my friends why it was bad.
   d. tell my friends to go to church more.

Eric Liddell's Famous Decision. Read the story and answer the questions below.

"... if anyone serves Me, him My Father will honor."
John 12:26b

It was 1924! Athletes from all over the world traveled to Paris, France, to compete in the Olympics. Tension ran high as several Scots waited on the field to hear what Eric Liddell would do.

"I've made my decision," Eric told several Olympic officials. "I have chosen not to run in the 100 meter race on Sunday."

"But, Eric, all of Scotland is counting on you," said one official. "You can't let your countrymen down."

"I know that my decision will disappoint the people of Scotland," Eric said. "But I can't run on the Lord's Day."

"Come on, Eric, what will people think? They'll laugh at you. And... what about your future?" replied another official.

"My future is with God. If a person knows a truth about God or has a conviction, then it would be wrong for him not to act on it. I will not run on Sunday."

Eric Liddell's decision was final. He did not run in the 100 meter that occurred on Sunday. Instead, he chose to run the 400 scheduled on another day and won a gold medal for Scotland.

1. What is a conviction? Use the context clues in the story and your glossary to write your own definition.

___

2. What was Eric Liddell's conviction? What was he willing give up to live out his conviction?

___

3. Read John 12:26. How did Eric Liddell serve God? How did God honor him?

___

4. What character quality helped Eric Liddell to stand against peer pressure? Shade in all the letters contained in his name to answer the question.

44

Joshua: The Leader   11

A

General Joshua Goes to War. Read the verses from Joshua. Write the answer to each question in the squares. Using the letters in the numbered squares, write the promise God gave to Joshua in each battle below.

1. The city where Joshua marched around and blew horns. (6:1-5) — **Jericho**
2. The city where Joshua held out his spear to capture it. (8:18) — **Ai**
3. The city where Joshua commanded the sun to stand still. (10:12) — **Gibeon**
4. The city where Joshua discovered five kings in a cave. (10:15-17) — **Makkedah**
5. The place where Joshua tied the hamstrings of horses. (11:5-6) — **Waters of Merom**

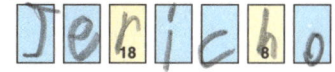

God's promise to Joshua in each battle was:

"**I have given them into your hands.**"

B

Being a Good Soldier. Read 2 Timothy 2:3-4 and finish the sentences to find out how you can serve God better as a soldier. (Clue: Find one thing you must do and one thing you must not do).

We must choose to _____ as a "good soldier." (v. 3)

We must choose not to become engaged in _____ _____ . (v. 4)

Whom does a "good soldier" choose to please? _____ . (v. 4)

Name one thing you can choose to do this week that shows you're a "good soldier."

_____

45

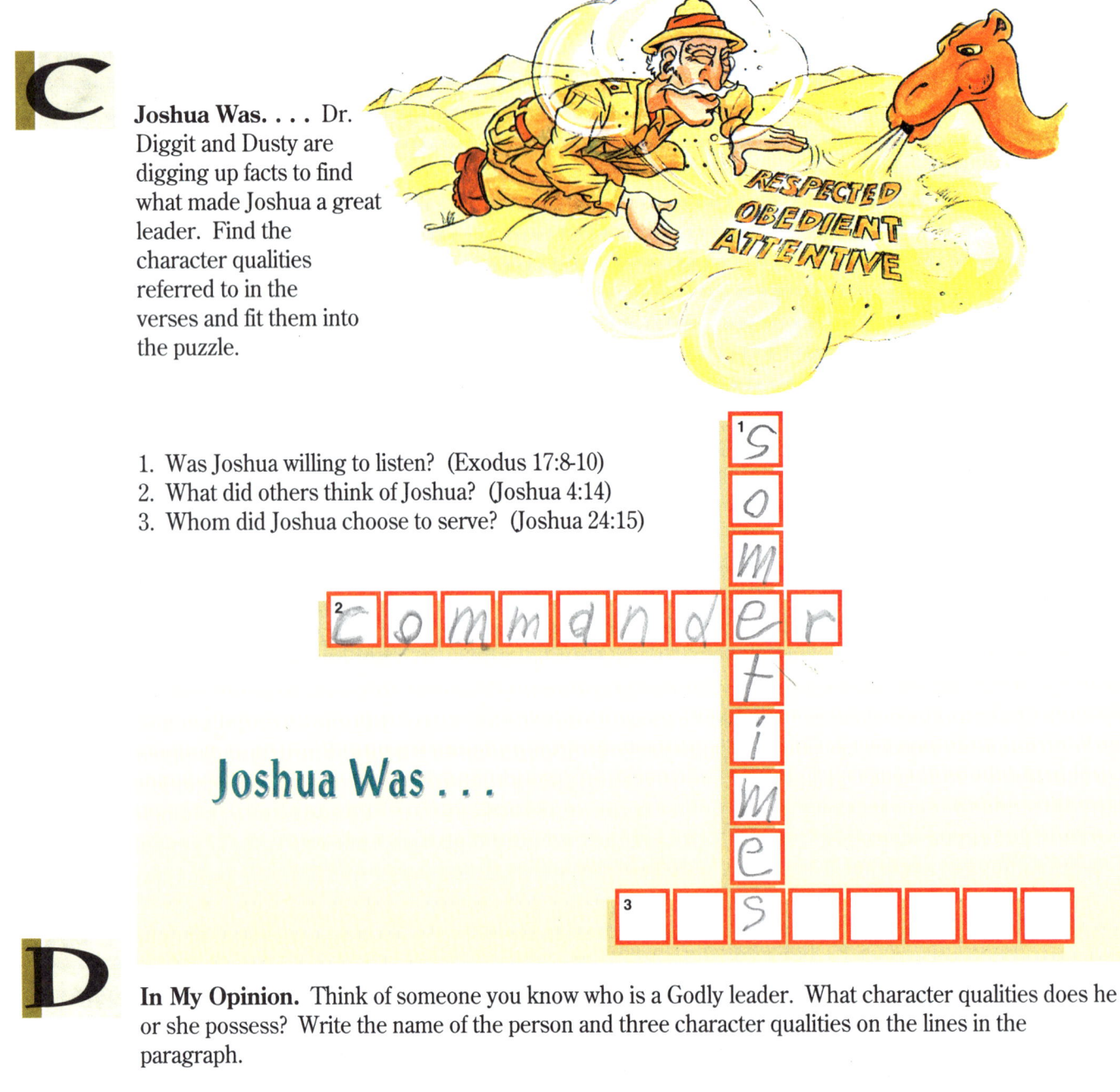

Joshua Was. . . . Dr. Diggit and Dusty are digging up facts to find what made Joshua a great leader. Find the character qualities referred to in the verses and fit them into the puzzle.

1. Was Joshua willing to listen? (Exodus 17:8-10)
2. What did others think of Joshua? (Joshua 4:14)
3. Whom did Joshua choose to serve? (Joshua 24:15)

Joshua Was . . .

1. S
   O
   M
2. C O M M A N D E R
   T
   I
   M
   E
3. _ _ S _ _ _ _ _

In My Opinion. Think of someone you know who is a Godly leader. What character qualities does he or she possess? Write the name of the person and three character qualities on the lines in the paragraph.

In my opinion _____ is a Godly leader because he/she is 1. _____,

2. _____ and 3. _____.

Give examples of his/her leadership qualities.

1. _____

2. _____

3. _____

Be prepared to share the quality you most admire!

E **Joshua's Secret of Success.** Austin, Katie and Dr. Diggit are having an interesting discussion about Joshua's success. Using the verses from Joshua, complete the conversation to find God's formula for success. Then answer the question.

Well, Joshua was successful because he _____ all the _____. (1:7)

But Joshua was also successful because he *meditated* on the Word *day* and *night*. (1:8)

And don't forget that Joshua was careful to _____ (1:8) everything written in God's Word.

The secret to Joshua's success was that he _____
_____

F **What Is Godly Meditation?** Use your glossary to look up the definition of **meditation**. Describe in one sentence what it means to meditate on God's Word.

_____
_____

Below are some ways people meditate on God's Word. See if you can add a few ideas to the list.

Reading the Bible   _____

Thinking about verses   _____

Writing verses out   _____

_____   _____

G **Israel's Idols.** God knew how important it was for His people to learn to say "No!" to sin. Read the verses and circle **T** for true and **F** for false. Correct the answers that are false by drawing lines through the words to make the statement true.

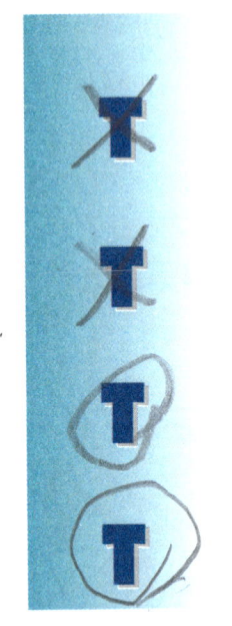

~~T~~ • The Lord commanded that all the nations be put to death except for the Canaanites. (Deuteronomy 20:17) **F**

~~T~~ • God said He would not drive out the other nations because of their horrible practices. (Deuteronomy 18:12) **F**

T • God's reason for wanting to destroy the other nations was so that they wouldn't teach Israel their evil practices. (Deuteronomy 20:18) ~~F~~

T • God did not want Israel to get involved in the evil practices of sacrificing children, witchcraft, and other things. (Deuteronomy 18:10) ~~F~~

Put a star by the statement that tells why God wanted Israel to kill all the inhabitants of the land.

H **Our Idols?** Can we have a problem with idolatry? Sure! Whenever we put something ahead of God in our lives, we are in danger of idolatry too. Check the statements that are true about you.

I often long for new bikes, games or other things.

I get envious when I see friends wearing new clothes.

I dream about living in a big house like some of my friends.

I constantly wish I was as pretty or handsome as some of my classmates.

I neglect doing other important things to play sports better than my friend.

Read Colossians 3:5 and answer the question.

Why are the items on the checklist above similar to idolatry?
_____
_____

48

Achan: Hiding Sin

12

A

Surprise at Ai. Read Joshua 7 and follow the directions.

1. Describe how Israel felt when they lost the battle at Ai. (vs. 4-5)

   _____

   _____

2. Joshua asked God three questions after Israel's defeat at Ai. His questions show concern for three different groups of people. On the lines write the word from each question that tells who Joshua was concerned about. (vs. 6-9)

   ...Lord God, why have You brought this people over the Jordan...to destroy us?

   O Lord, what can I say now that Israel has been routed by its enemies?

   The other nations will hear about this, Lord, and then what will You do for Your great name?

B

Getting God's Bigger Picture. Read Joshua 7:10-11 and answer the questions.

Did Joshua know why Israel was defeated? Yes. _____ No. _____

Did Israel know why they were defeated? Yes. _____ No. _____

Did God know why Israel was defeated? Yes. _____ No. _____

Why was Israel defeated in the battle at Ai? _____

What is true about God that enables Him to know everything?
(Use the circle code to write the answer.)

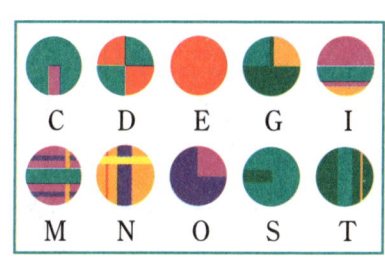

49

C **The Big Sin in Israel.** Using Joshua 7, fill in the blanks.

1. Why was Israel defeated in Ai?

The Children of Israel could not stand before their _____ (v.13) because they had

committed _____ (v. 1) by regarding the _____ (v.1) things. God said that

Israel had _____ (v. 11)

2. Israel had sinned in at least five areas. (v. 11) List the specific sins on the lines in the five links.

3. What choice did Israel have to make for God to continue with them? (7:12)

_____

D **The Big Burial in Achor.** Achan's sin had grave consequences for not only himself but also for the people he loved. Read Joshua 7:24 and shade in all the people, animals and things that were buried beneath the stones with Achan. (Hint: Words can go in angles).

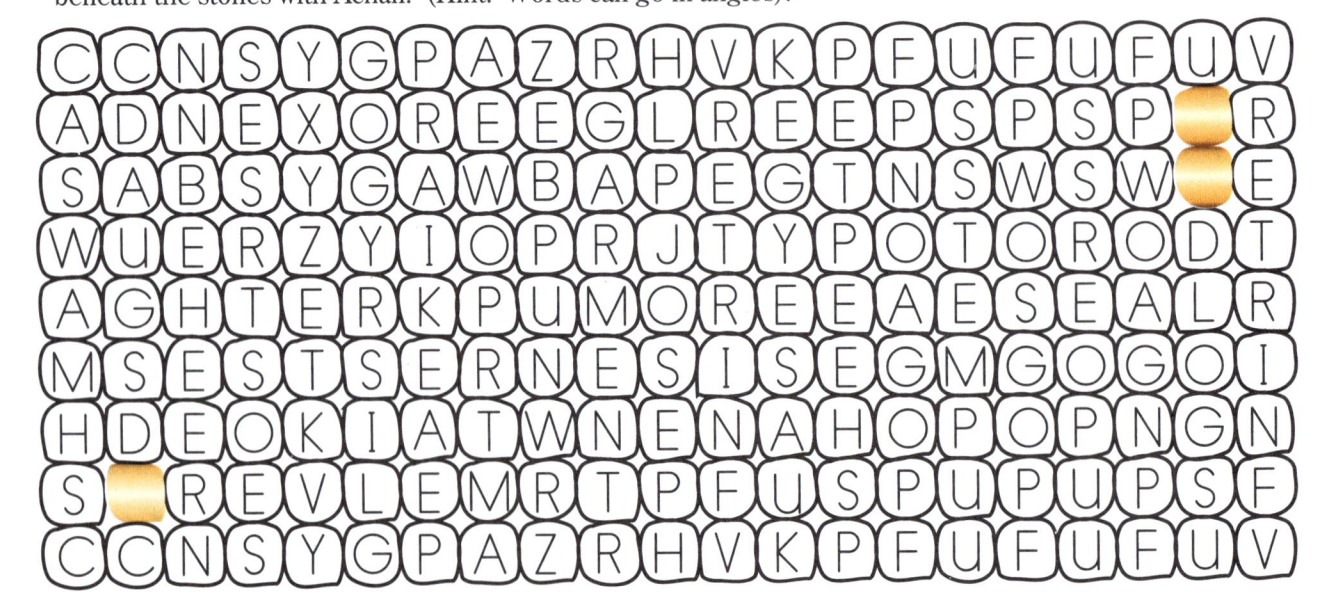

50

12

E **Dealing with Stealing.** Austin and Katie have figured out that people can steal other things besides material possessions. Read the case studies that follow and respond to the questions. Use the Word Bank and Scripture Bank for your answers. (One word and reference will not be used.)

Word Bank

someone's time
someone's reputation
someone's property
someone's money

Scripture Bank

Colossians 4:5
James 5:8
Ephesians 4:28
James 4:11

Case Study #1:

Mrs. Troxel had asked her fifth grade class to follow her down the hall to the library without talking. She kept hearing several students behind her laughing and giggling, but she couldn't tell who was doing it. Mrs. Troxel turned around twice to ask who was talking, but no one said anything. Finally she told the class that they would miss some of their recess time because of the disruption.

What is being stolen? _____ Which reference fits? _____

Case Study #2:

On the way to school Mike had overheard Benjamin telling some other boys that he had lost his baseball mitt the day before. While Mike was on the playground at recess, he found a baseball mitt with no name written in it in the bushes. Mike thought, "This could be Ben's baseball mitt, but…it really doesn't have a name on it. And besides, Ben really didn't tell me he had lost it. I think I'll keep it."

What is being stolen? _____ Which reference fits? _____

Case Study #3:

Mary commented to her friend at lunchtime that Julie, another classmate, had worn an ugly dress with dirty tennis shoes to school. Lanie overheard the comment and turned to Sue to tell her what Mary had said about Julie.

What is being stolen? _____ Which reference fits? _____

F The "Blind Poetess."

Have you ever wondered what it would be like if you were blind? Would you have a harder time learning in school? Would you feel cheated? Fanny Crosby was blind from the time she was six weeks old. And learning was more difficult for her, but she didn't feel cheated. She learned to be content with her blindness and became one of the greatest Christian hymn writers of all times.

At an early age Fanny began writing poetry and memorizing whole books of the Bible. Under the influence of her grandmother and a family friend, Mrs. Hawley, Fanny memorized over seven books of the Bible by the time she was ten. When she was in her teens, she was sent away to attend a school for the blind. At school, her love for God's Word and poetry began to grow. She wrote poems for many occasions and became known as the "Blind Poetess."

Fanny Crosby wrote over 8,000 hymns during her lifetime. The hymns she wrote tell what she thought about the Lord, what she thought about her life and what was most important to her. One day a gentleman complained to her about being poor. He said things like, "If I were wealthy, I wouldn't have any more problems." Fanny couldn't stop thinking about what the man had said. She went right home and wrote a song that expressed what she thought about the world's riches. She named the song, "Give Me Jesus."

Give Me Jesus

Take the world, but give me Jesus, All its joys are but a name;
But His love abideth ever, Thru eternal years the same.

Take the world, but give me Jesus, Sweetest comfort of my soul;
With my Savior watching o'er me, I can sing tho' billows roll.

Take the world, but give me Jesus, Let me view His constant smile;
Then throughout my pilgrim journey, Light will cheer me all the while.

Take the world, but give me Jesus, In His cross my trust shall be;
Till, with clearer, brighter vision, Face to face my Lord I see.

Use the lyrics above to answer these questions.

1. What did Fanny Crosby want most in life? _____

2. Circle the phrase that shows she believed in a "God who sees."

3. Draw a box around the words that are related to seeing.

4. Underline the sentence that shows what she trusted.

5. Put a wavy line under what she chose to give up.

Overview of Judges: Cycle of Sin

A   Checking Out the Cycles.
Read the verses in Judges and put a check in the circles where you see the following:

> Ohoooo..., I think all these circles and cycles are making me dizzy!

	Sinfulness	Suffering	Supplications	Solutions
3:7-9	●	●	●	●
3:12-15	●	●	●	●
4:1-3	●	●	●	●
6:1-2, 7-8	●	●	●	●
10:6-10; 11:29	●	●	●	●
13:1-5	●	●	●	●

B   Going Around in Cycles.
Israel chose to make the same mistakes again and again. To find the cycle in Judges, begin at **Start**, draw a line through the maze and end in the middle. Write the letters you cross through on the spaces to the side. (The letters will make four words.)

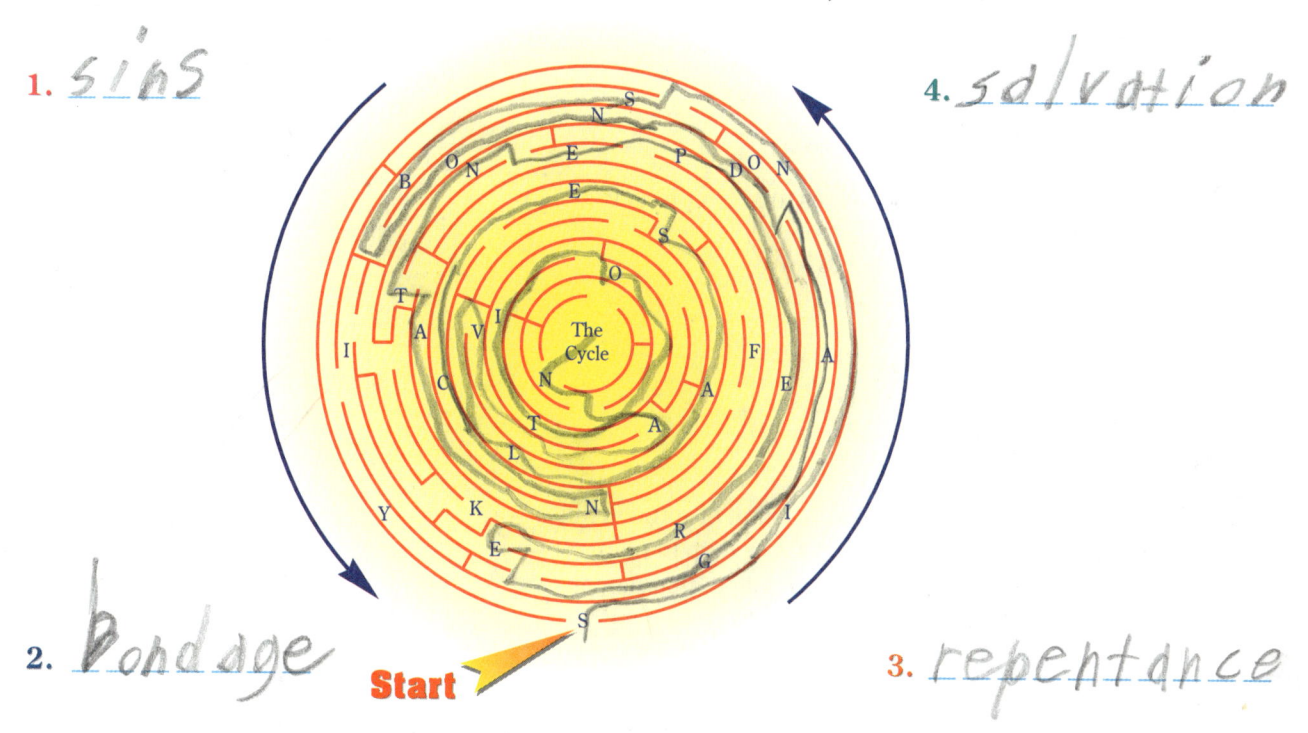

1. sins
2. bondage
3. repentance
4. salvation

Start

53

C

Who Were Israel's Judges? Dr. Diggit, Austin and Katie are beginning a Bible search to find out something about Israel's judges. Read the verses in Judges and list their names on the lines. Draw a line matching the judge to the correct fact. Then answer the question below.

The Judges

3:9 _____
3:15 _____
3:31 _____
4:4 _____
6:12 _____
10:1 _____
10:3-4 _____
11:29-30 _____
12:8-9 _____
12:11 _____
12:13-14 _____
15:20; 16:6 _____

The Facts

the Zebulunite

saw the "angel..."

tribe of Issachar

made a vow to God

had great strength

controlled 30 cities

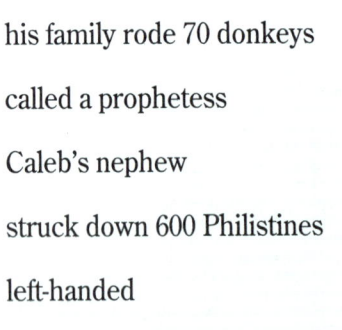

his family rode 70 donkeys

called a prophetess

Caleb's nephew

struck down 600 Philistines

left-handed

30 sons / 30 daughters

Why did God raise up judges to help in Israel? (2:18)

_____
_____
_____

D

Who Are Your "Judges?" Think of someone in your own life whom God has raised up to help you. Complete the thank-you note to that person.

Dear _____,
I want to thank you for ministering to me by _____
_____
_____
_____
_____
_____

13

E **The Father's Grace.** Read Luke 15:11-32 and work the crossword puzzle. Then work with a partner to answer the questions below on notebook paper.

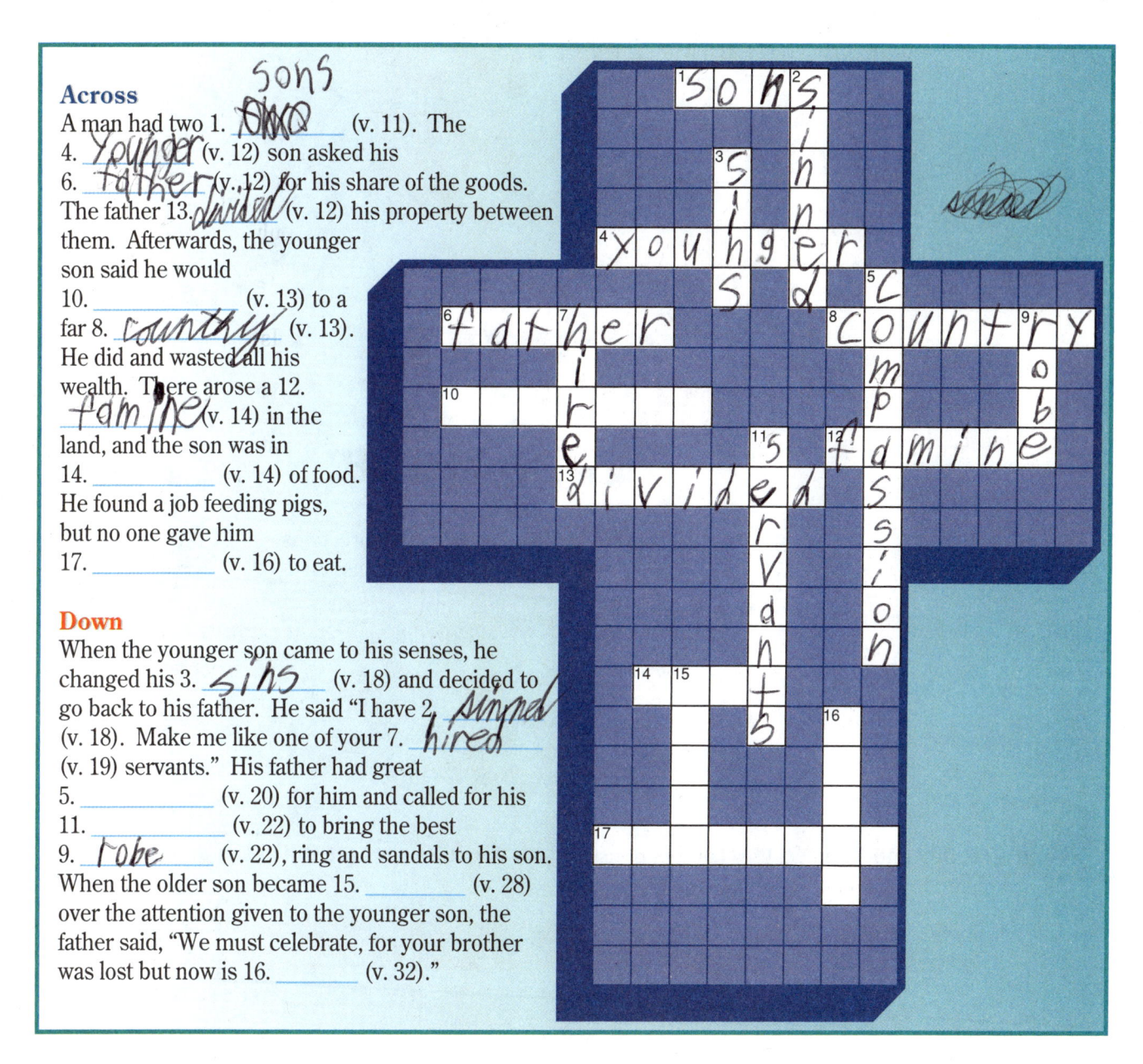

Across
A man had two 1. ~~two~~ sons (v. 11). The 4. younger (v. 12) son asked his 6. father (v. 12) for his share of the goods. The father 13. divided (v. 12) his property between them. Afterwards, the younger son said he would 10. _____ (v. 13) to a far 8. country (v. 13). He did and wasted all his wealth. There arose a 12. famine (v. 14) in the land, and the son was in 14. _____ (v. 14) of food. He found a job feeding pigs, but no one gave him 17. _____ (v. 16) to eat.

Down
When the younger son came to his senses, he changed his 3. sins (v. 18) and decided to go back to his father. He said "I have 2. sinned (v. 18). Make me like one of your 7. hired (v. 19) servants." His father had great 5. _____ (v. 20) for him and called for his 11. _____ (v. 22) to bring the best 9. robe (v. 22), ring and sandals to his son. When the older son became 15. _____ (v. 28) over the attention given to the younger son, the father said, "We must celebrate, for your brother was lost but now is 16. _____ (v. 32)."

1. Why did the son change his mind and return to his father?

2. What was the father's attitude toward the son?

3. How did the father in the parable show grace to his son?

4. How is God's grace like the father's?

F **The RULES Game.** Follow all the directions and answer all the questions.

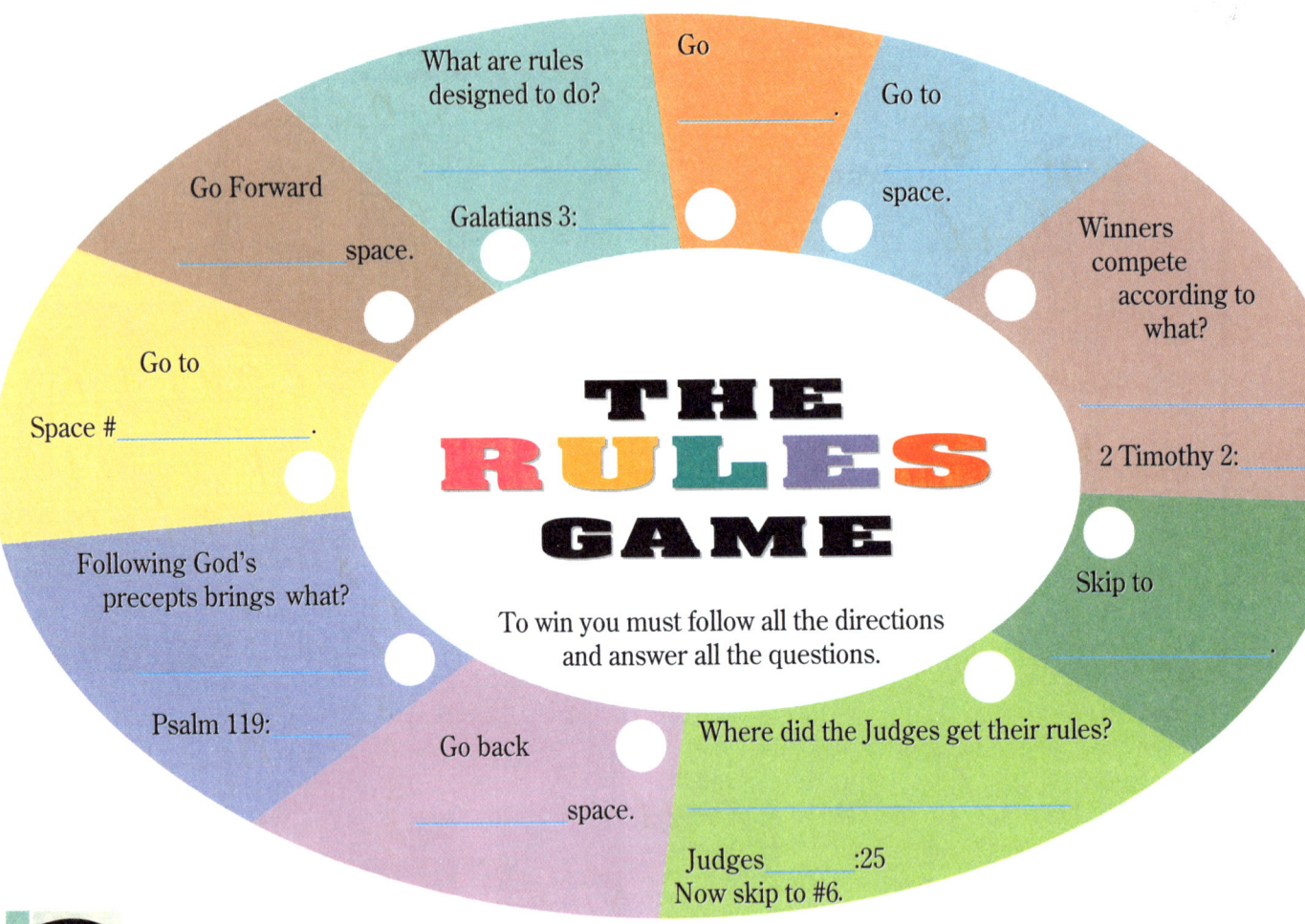

THE RULES GAME

To win you must follow all the directions and answer all the questions.

- What are rules designed to do? Galatians 3: _____
- Go _____.
- Go to _____ space.
- Winners compete according to what? 2 Timothy 2: _____
- Skip to _____.
- Where did the Judges get their rules? Judges _____ :25. Now skip to #6.
- Go back _____ space.
- Psalm 119: _____ Following God's precepts brings what?
- Go to Space # _____.
- Go Forward _____ space.

G **Rules and You.** On the chart below list two or three rules you have at home or at school. Then list the purpose and benefit of these rules.

The Rule	Purpose	Benefit

Deborah: A Helper to Others   14

A

Viewing Deborah's World. Dr. Diggit is on another expedition to find out what life was like in Deborah's day. Read the verses in the Book of Judges and cross out the incorrect word in the facts below.

The Children of Israel were. . . (4:1-3)
 doing good/evil in God's sight.
 sold into Jabin's/Lapidoth's hand.
 ruled by the Moabites/Canaanites.
 treated harshly/wonderfully.
 oppressed for thirty/twenty years.

Israel's cities and towns were. . . (5:6-8)
 filled with activity/inactivity.
 crowded/empty on the highways.
 overflowing with people carrying/not carrying weapons.

B

Describing Deborah's World. Imagine you are an historian writing a summary about what Israel was like in the days of Deborah. Use the facts you found in Exercise A to complete a brief description.

In the days of Deborah, Israel _____

_____

_____

_____

C

Juggling Jobs. Deborah was a very busy lady! In fact, she had three jobs. Read Judges 4:4 and unscramble the words below that tell what her three jobs were. Then fill in the meaning of her name.

disalhotp fiwe _____ _____ _____ _____ _____ , _____ _____ _____ _____

ortpepshse _____ _____ _____ _____ _____ _____ _____ _____

duegj _____ _____ _____ _____ _____

Deborah's name means. . .
" _____ "   + 🦫 -VER

Why was Deborah a fitting name? _____

57

D **Looks Impossible!** Have you ever needed a friend to help you trust the Lord in a tough situation? Well, that's just what Barak needed. See if you can tell who made the difference. Read the verses in Judges and follow directions.

1. Compare the war weapons of Jabin and the Canaanites with those in Israel. (4:3 and 5:8)

   _____

   _____

   Based on the weaponry, who was more likely to win the battle? _____

2. Fill in the conversation between Deborah and Barak. (4:6-9)

   (vs. 6-7)   (v. 8)   (v. 14)

Why do you think Barak did not want to go to war without Deborah?

He was too scared he was going to die.

E **But. . . It Was Possible!** Read the verses and answer Austin and Katie's questions.

Why did the weather help to win the battle?

Answer: (5:4, 21) _____

Who made the difference in Barak's life and helped him trust God?

Answer: (4:14) _____

_____

_____

14

F. Singing "Deborah's Song."
When the Canaanites were defeated Deborah and Barak sang a song of praise. Read the verses in Judges 5 and answer the questions.

Deborah praised God for what two things? (5:2)

1. _____

2. _____

Whom did Deborah praise for the victory? (5:4-5) _____

What did Deborah pray for those who love God? (5:31) _____

_____

G. Praising Wise Leaders.
Read Judges 5:14-18. List the groups who chose to help and the ones who did not. Write the numbers in the circles to show what the groups chose to do instead of helping.

Groups Who Chose To Help	Groups Who Chose Not To Help
_____	○ _____
_____	○ _____
_____	○ _____
_____	○ _____

1. Chose to stay on the ships   3. Chose to stay with sheep
2. Chose to stay on the coast   4. Chose to stay near Jordan

H. Depending on God and Others.
Deborah depended on help from two sources. Write them on the scales. Now place a star beside the One she depended on the most. (Hint: You can depend on Him, too.)

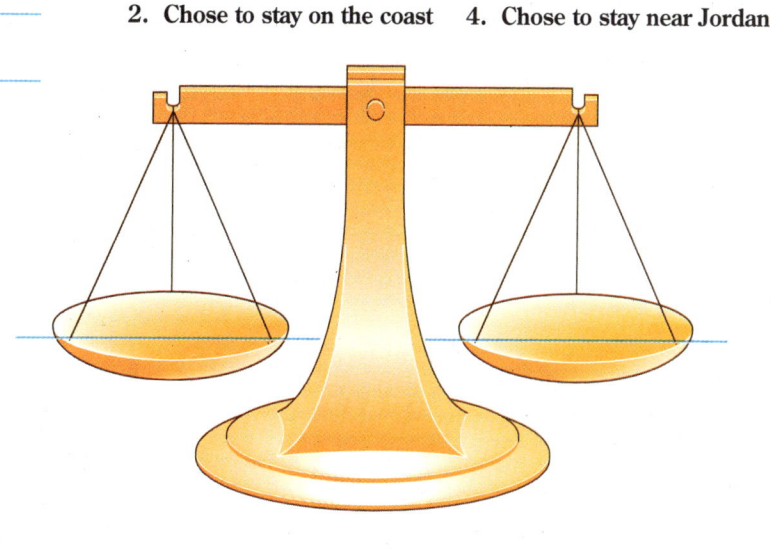

I God Helps Me. Read the following list of truths about your "Helper." Match the truth with a correct reference from the verse bank.

> **Verse Bank**
> Psalm 30:10   Hebrews 13:6   Psalm 54:1-4   Psalm 124:8
> Romans 8:26   Psalm 121:2   Psalm 46:1-2

The Truth	Verse
My help comes from the Lord.	_____
My help is in the name of the Lord.	_____
God is my help in time of trouble.	_____
I can pray for the Lord to be my helper.	_____
God is my helper, so I won't fear.	_____
God the Spirit helps me know how to pray.	_____
God helps me to endure.	_____

Go back and put a check by the truth that has helped you the most. Then give a reason for your choice.

_____

J I Help Others. Decode the puzzle below to find out how you can help other people.

A	B	D	E
G	H	I	L
N	O	R	S
	T	U	
	6	2	

60

Gideon: A Man Who Faced Fear

15

A. A Dreary Diary.
Pretend you are an Israelite living in Gideon's day. Record 1150 B.C. by the date. Then read Judges 6:2-5. Write a description in your diary of what life was like when the Midianites came through your village.

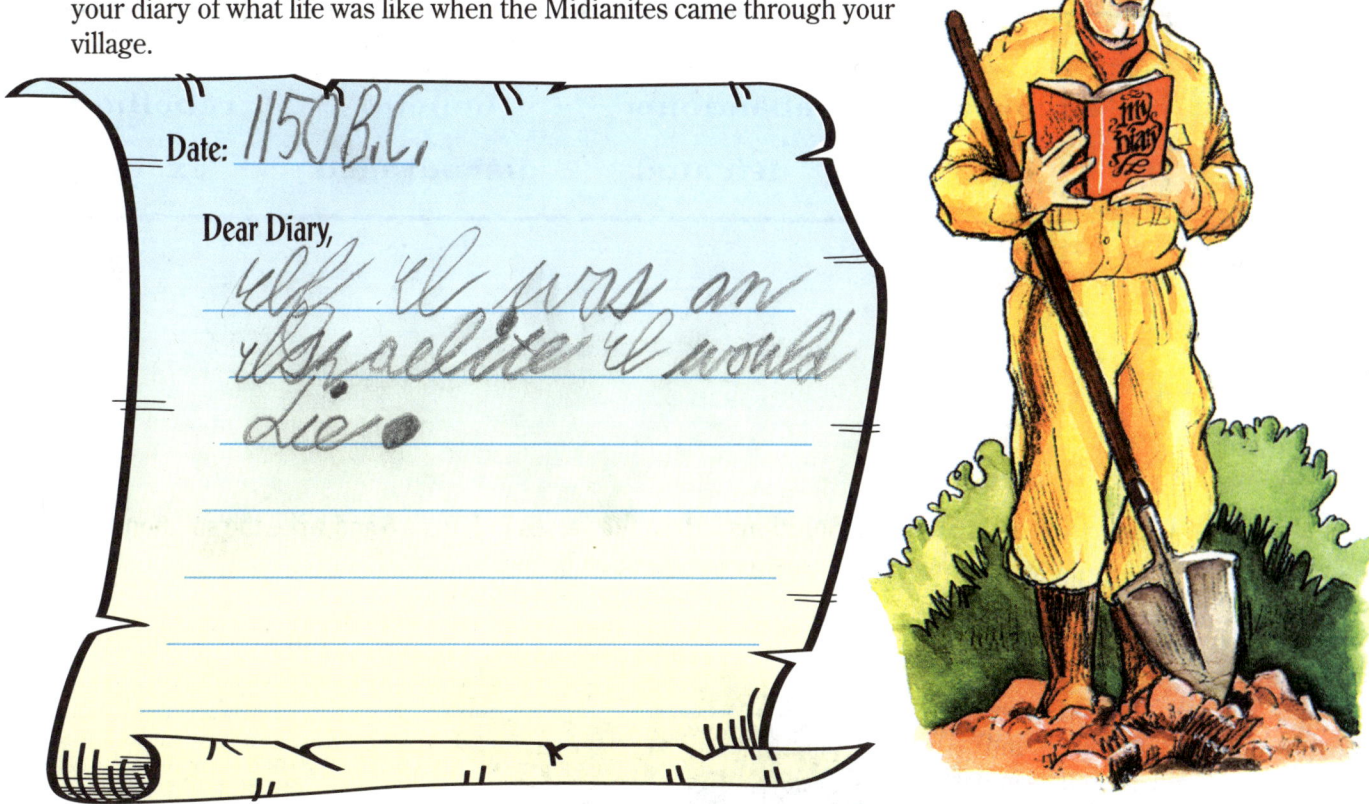

Date: 1150 B.C.

Dear Diary,

If I was an Israelite I would die.

B. A Prophet's Pronouncement.
Read Judges 6:8-10 and answer the questions.

What acts of God did the prophet remind Israel?

(v. 8) _____

(v. 9) _____

Which of God's commands did the prophet repeat to Israel?

(v. 10) _____

What reason did the prophet give for Israel's oppression? Circle every third letter to find the reason and write it on the line below.

A B I C K S R D R Q E A L S E O P L G V D K E I E F S
B K O P L B N G E D H Y U J E R H D C T G L U O A R D

_____

61

C **Gideon's Feelings.** Read Judges 6:13. Circle three words that describe how Gideon felt. Then write a sentence for each word telling how the word describes Gideon's feelings.

> **Word Bank**
>
> encouraged   abandoned   hopeful   rebellious
>
> angry   defeated   discouraged   excited

❶ _____
❷ _____
❸ _____

D **Gideon's Fears . . . God's Solutions.** Read the verses in Judges 6 and write the solution the Angel of the Lord gave to Gideon. Then answer the question below.

Gideon said . . .

"The Lord has forsaken us and delivered us into the hands of the Midianites." (v. 13)

"My clan is the weakest . . . and I am the least in my father's house." (v. 15)

"... show me a sign that it is You Who talks with me." (v. 17)

but God's solution was . . .

_____
_____
_____ (v. 14)

_____
_____
_____ (v. 16)

_____
_____ (v. 21)

What did Gideon's objections show about his faith? Explain. _____
_____
_____

15

E **Too Many Men!** Austin and Katie need help with these math story problems. Read the verses in Judges and fill in the blanks with the correct numbers. (Clue: #2 is tricky.)

❶ If there were _____ people from the East and _____ (8:10) men who drew their swords, how many Midianites were there in all? _____

❷ If there were _____ people who returned because they were fearful and _____ (7:3) who remained, but God chose only the _____ who lapped like a dog, how many were left in Israel's army to fight the Midianites? _____ (7:6)

How many men did God send home? _____

❸ If there were _____ in the Midianite army and _____ were left in the Israelite army, how many more people were in the Midianite army than in Israel's?

_____

F **Scrambled Events.** Read Judges 7:16-25. Unscramble the ten events below by numbering them in the order they took place. Then answer the question.

_____ Israel held torches up in the air.
_____ Israel broke the pitchers.
_____ Israel went after the Midianites.
_____ Israel blew trumpets.
_____ The Midianites fled to Beth Acacia.
_____ Ephraim's men took over the watering places.
_____ Gideon divided his men into three companies.
_____ Gideon instructed his men to do as he did.
_____ Israel captured the Midianite princes, Oreb and Zeeb.
_____ Israel cried, "The sword of the Lord and of Gideon."

What is our "Sword of the Lord?" How can we choose to use it to fight our fears? (Ephesians 6:17)

_____
_____
_____

63

G **Key to the Hebrews Heroes.** The people in Hebrews 11:32-34 have something in common. Read the verses and list their names on the lines. When you discover what they had in common, write the word in big letters in the key and decorate it with color.

_____   _____   _____

_____   _____

H **Faith Is . . . Out of Sight.** We need to overcome fear by trusting in God and His Word. Draw a line matching the fear to the faith. Then read the verses and write a reference by the key which you think best fits the situation. Verses: Psalm 56:11; Psalm 115:11; 2 Timothy 2:15; Psalm 33:11; Romans 8:28.

The Fear

Billy is fearful he will fail the math test even after he has studied, then. . .

Kim is afraid to attend class wearing new glasses because she doesn't want her friends to laugh, then. . .

Randy becomes frightened in rainstorms when lightning and thunder are present, then. . .

Jan is fearful that her family might not stay together because they don't get along, then. . .

Kyle is afraid that the world is going to be ruined with pollution, then. . .

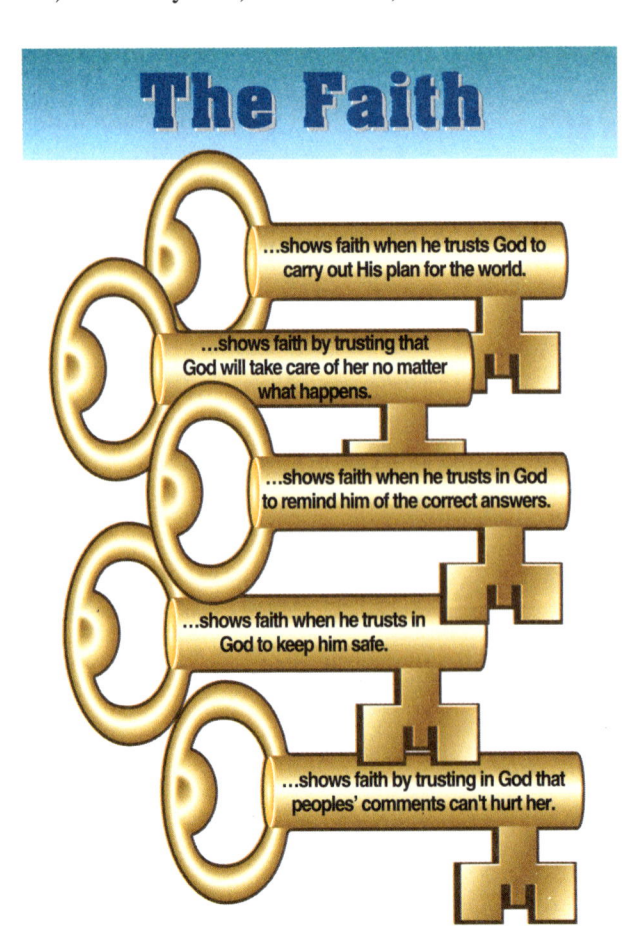

The Faith

. . .shows faith when he trusts God to carry out His plan for the world.

. . .shows faith by trusting that God will take care of her no matter what happens.

. . .shows faith when he trusts in God to remind him of the correct answers.

. . .shows faith when he trusts in God to keep him safe.

. . .shows faith by trusting in God that peoples' comments can't hurt her.

Jephthah: Overcoming a Poor Background — 16

A

Mixed-Up 'N Mixed-In. Dr. Diggit has just made a list of some of the pagan gods and goddesses in Jephthah's day. Read Judges 10:6. List the people group who worshiped those idols in the order they appear in Scripture. (The first three have been done for you.) To answer the question about Israel's worship, shade in the scrambled letters in the picture that spell all the people groups.

False Gods	People Groups
Baal and Asherah	Canaanites
Baal	Syria
Baal and Astarte	Sidon
Chemosh	*Moab*
Molech	*Ammon*
Dagon	*Philistines*

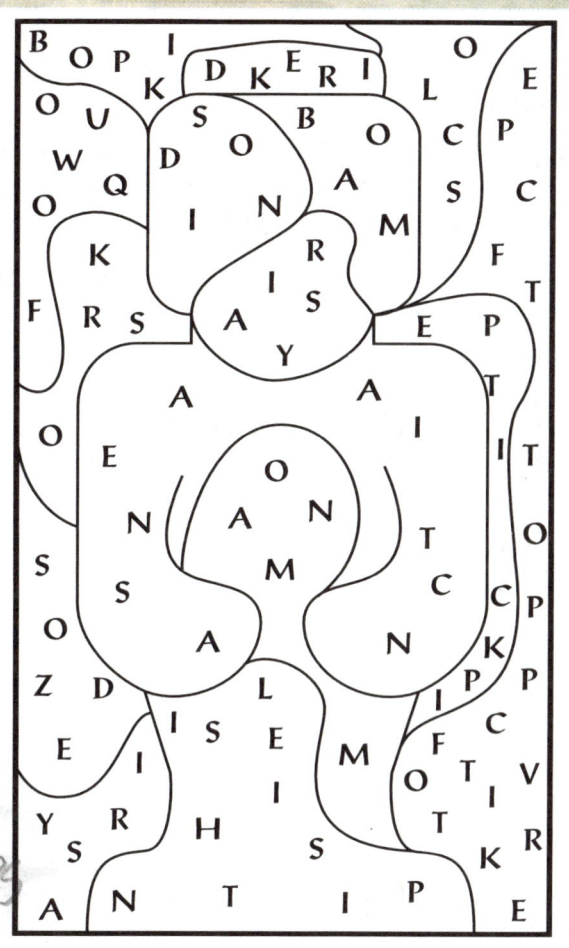

Why was Israel mixed-up and what was mixed in with Israel's worship?

Israel disobeyed God and worshiped other Gods.

B

Real Repentance . . . Really! God wasn't willing to forgive Israel until He saw real repentance. Read Judges 10:15-16 and write what Israel did to show God their repentance was real.

> Remember, real repentance is not just feeling sorrow for your sins. It's choosing to change your mind and actions too!

Israel confessed _*their sins*_.

Israel was willing to take _*God's punishment*_.

Israel destroyed _*the idols*_.

Israel served _*the Lord*_.

C   **The "Bad Apple."** Help Austin and Katie find out why Jephthah's family thought of him as the "bad apple" in the family. Read the verses in Judges 11 and write all the information you can find about each family member. (Clue: You will not find information on one member.) Then answer the question and give a reason.

Jephthah's Family Tree

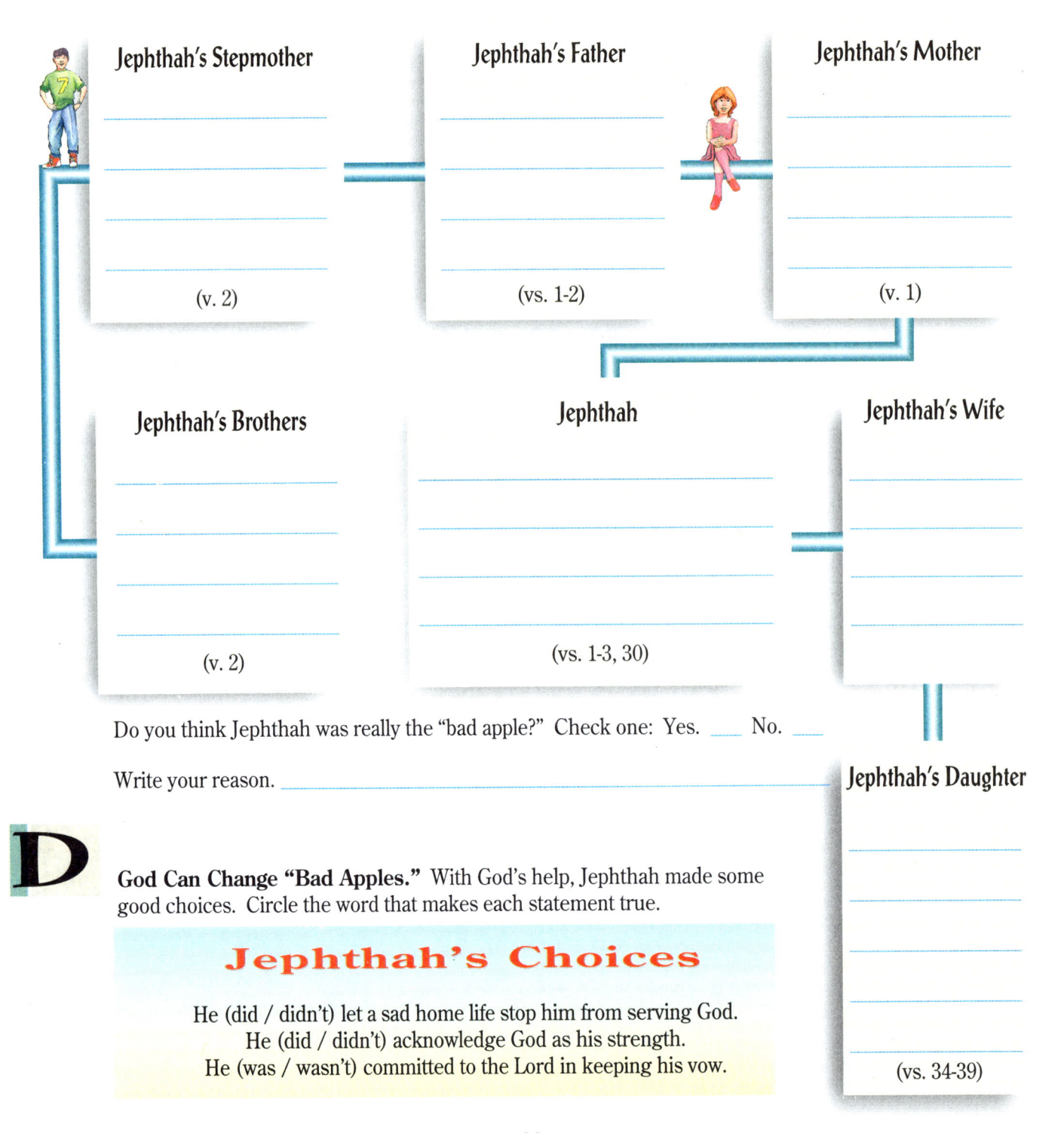

Jephthah's Stepmother
(v. 2)

Jephthah's Father
(vs. 1-2)

Jephthah's Mother
(v. 1)

Jephthah's Brothers
(v. 2)

Jephthah
(vs. 1-3, 30)

Jephthah's Wife

Jephthah's Daughter
(vs. 34-39)

Do you think Jephthah was really the "bad apple?" Check one: Yes. ___ No. ___

Write your reason. _____

D   **God Can Change "Bad Apples."** With God's help, Jephthah made some good choices. Circle the word that makes each statement true.

Jephthah's Choices

He (did / didn't) let a sad home life stop him from serving God.
He (did / didn't) acknowledge God as his strength.
He (was / wasn't) committed to the Lord in keeping his vow.

16

E A Hasty Vow = A Bad Decision.
The pictures below show what happened when Jephthah made his vow to the Lord. Read the verses in Judges 11 and write a title for each picture in the shaded boxes. Then in the speech bubbles, write in your own words what the characters said or what they might have said.

Speech bubble (vs. 30-31): "Yes Lord I will!!!"

(vs. 30-31)

(vs. 32-33)

(v. 34)

(vs. 35-39)

F Was It Good or Bad?
Read the verses and answer the questions. Be sure to check whether you think Jephthah's choice was good or bad.

Why did Jephthah choose to keep the vow he had made even when it caused pain to his daughter and him? (11:35)

_____

_____ Good _____ or Bad _____ ?

What was the real reason Jephthah made the vow? (11:30-31)

_____

_____ Good _____ or Bad _____ ?

67

Interview with a Vow-Maker. Have you ever wondered what Jephthah would have said about vows after his experience? Pretend you are Jephthah being interviewed by a commentator on television. Use the verses and your glossary to fill in what you think Jephthah would have said.

Interviewer: Judge Jephthah, I understand that besides being a judge, you are also a vow-maker. First, tell us . . . just what is a vow?

Jephthah: (use glossary) _____
_____
_____
_____

Interviewer: Judge, can you give us a little historical background about how vow-making got started?

Jephthah: (Numbers 30:1-2) _____
_____
_____
_____

Interviewer: Judge, as you know, the vow you made concerning your daughter has been a much publicized event. Tell us, did someone force you into making that vow or was this something you decided on your own?

Jephthah: (Deuteronomy 23:22-23) _____
_____

Interviewer: But Mr. Jephthah, when you saw that the decision you had made was going to affect your daughter for life, why didn't you just back out?

Jephthah: (Ecclesiastes 5:4-5) _____
_____
_____
_____

Interviewer: Judge Jephthah, if you could give one piece of advice to all the vow-makers of this world, what would it be?

Jephthah: (Ecclesiastes 5:2) _____
_____
_____
_____

Interviewer: Judge, thank you for being on our program today. And thank you, ladies and gentlemen, for tuning in with us today.

Better not to vow than to vow and not pay.
Ecclesiastes 5:5

Samson: Wrong Choices

17

A **Truly . . . "The Angel."** Manoah and his wife were very excited when they realized the Angel of the Lord was announcing their son's birth. Read Judges 13:3-20. If the statement is true, circle the letter under T. If it is false, circle the letter under F. Then write the circled letters in order, matching the numbers in the boxes, to find out who the Angel really was.

The Angel said to Samson's mother...   T   F

1. You will have a daughter.   F   Ⓙ
2. Don't drink wine.   Ⓔ   A
3. Your son will deliver Israel from Moab. T Ⓢ
4. Take a razor and cut his hair.   V   Ⓤ
5. Your son will be a Nazarite.   Ⓢ   P

The Angel said to Samson's father...   T   F

6. I will sit and eat with you.   K   Ⓒ
7. Your wife will not eat anything unclean. Ⓗ A
8. Go live in another land.   P   Ⓡ
9. Your wife can drink similar drinks to wine. T Ⓘ
10. Don't offer a burnt offering to the Lord. C Ⓢ
11. My name...it is wonderful.   Ⓣ   P

1	2	3	4	5	6	7	8	9	10	11
J	e	s	u	s	C	h	r	i	s	t

B **The Vow of a Nazarite.** Read Numbers 6:2-8 and in the open scroll write the three things a Nazarite must do. Then write a definition of a Nazarite.

A Nazarite must ...

1. _not cut his hair._ (v. 3)
2. _not drink wine._ (v. 5)
3. _touch dead bodies._ (v. 6)

Use Numbers 6:2, 8 and your glossary to complete the definition.

A Nazarite was a person who _is seperated from God._

C. Solve a Riddle.
Read the following verses and draw a line from the reference to the stanza that matches. Write in the missing word in each stanza, rhyming it with the last word in the second line to complete the riddle about Samson's strength.

Samson was a man of God;
His strength was simply grand.
He killed a roaring, raging lion
With nothing but his ___hands___.

Judges 16:2-3

The Gazites thought that Samson
Would be an easy catch.
But he escaped through city gates
Without lifting up the ___latch___.

Judges 16:30

The Philistines had bound Samson
But God's Spirit set him free.
He killed a thousand of their men
With the jawbone of a ___donkey___.

Judges 16:29-30

Samson's final awesome feat
Just wasn't idle braggin'.
He pushed the pillars to the ground
And crumbled the Temple of ___Dagon___.

Judges 15:15-17

Countless wicked people died –
The price for willful sin.
For if you're not on God's side,
There's no way you can ___win___.

Judges 14:5-6

D. Going Down!
Read the verses and answer the questions on the chart below.

What Does God Say?	What Did Samson Do?	Consequences of Sin
Deuteronomy 7:3-4	Judges 14:1-3	Judges 14:15 — Sin against God
Numbers 6:6	Judges 14:8-9	Clue: One sin led to another. What was it? — decieved his parents
Proverbs 7:5	Judges 16:1	Judges 16:17-21 — a slave

70

17

E **Samson's Last Stand.** God revealed His plan for Samson before he was even born. Use the code, 1 for the letter A, 2 for the letter B and so on to find God's plan for Samson. Then read Judges 13:5 to check your answer.

B E G I N   T O   D E L I V E R
2 5 7 9 14 20 15 4 5 12 9 22 5 18

I S R A E L   F R O M   T H E
9 19 18 1 5 12 6 18 15 13 20 8 5

P H I L I S T I N E S
16 8 9 12 9 19 20 9 14 5 19

How was Samson's last act in destroying the Temple of Dagon a fulfillment of God's plan for him?

_____

F **The After T-unic Shirt.** Samson seemed to make wiser choices in the last few hours of his life than he had done earlier. Read Judges 16:28 and design a T-unic shirt that describes Samson's attitude after he chose to do God's will by bringing down the Temple of Dagon.

Hmmm . . . is this a T. . . T. . . T . . . Tunic Shirt?

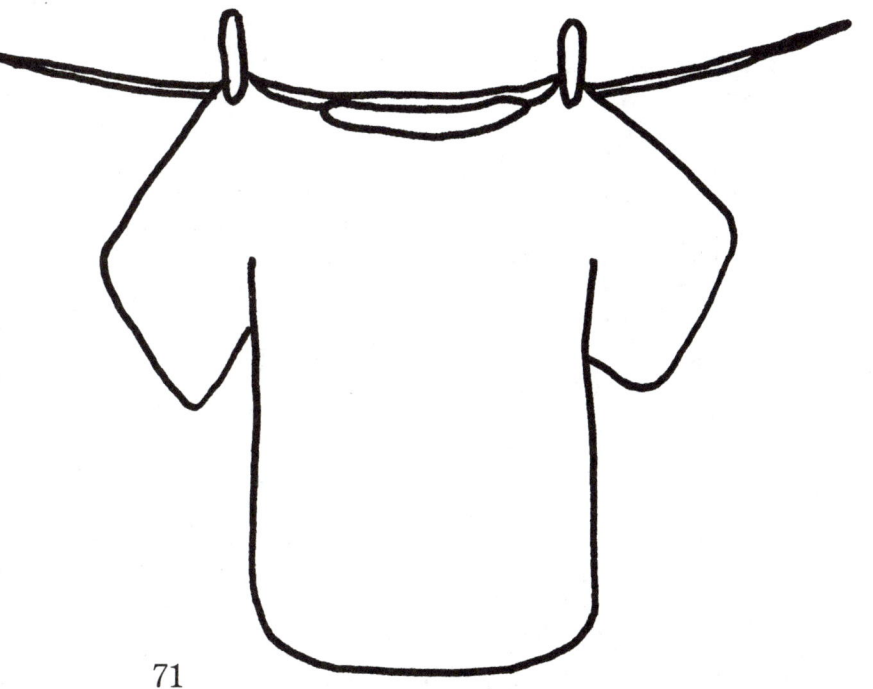

71

Holy Spirit Questions. Austin and Katie's friends have questions about the Holy Spirit. Use the information in the verses to write the answers to their questions.

"How does a person filled with the Holy Spirit act?" (Ephesians 5:18-21)

_____

_____

"The Bible can be so confusing. How are we supposed to understand it?" (John 16:12-13)

_____

_____

"How can I know for sure I am a child of God?" (Romans 8:16)

_____

_____

"How should I pray?" (Ephesians 6:18)

_____

_____

"What if I don't know what words to say when I pray?" (Romans 8:26)

_____

_____

"Why do I feel so bad when I do something wrong?" (John 16:7-8)

_____

_____

"How does a person grieve the Holy Spirit?" (Ephesians 4:25-32)

_____

_____

Ruth, Naomi and Boaz: Love and Loyalty

A

Three Suffered Losses. Have you ever lost something or someone who was very important to you? Naomi, Ruth and Orpah were three women who suffered great losses too. Read Ruth 1:1-5 and write what each lost. (Hint: One of the women suffered more than one loss.)

Naomi lost *husband and sons*.

Ruth lost *husband*.

Orpah lost *husband*.

B

Two Made Choices. Ruth and Orpah made different choices. Read Ruth 1:6-18. Write each name on the appropriate sign and list the pros and cons of each decision.

To Moab

Pros:

Cons:

To Bethlehem

Pros:

Cons:

How does God want you to respond when you lose something or someone who is important to you? Read Proverbs 3:5-6 and write your answer.

C **The Kinsman-Redeemer.** Using the verses and the word bank, complete the chart. When you are finished you will see an amazing likeness between Boaz, the kinsman-redeemer in Ruth's day, and Jesus Christ, the Kinsman-Redeemer in our day.

Word Bank

Me	Our Relatives	Adam
Mahlon	The Church	Boaz
Ruth	Another Close Relative	Jesus Christ

The Question	In Ruth's Day	In Our Day
Who was under a curse?	Hint: Who was the Moabitess? (Deuteronomy 23:3)	(Galatians 3:10)
Which relative died and left one who needed redemption?	(Ruth 1:4-5)	(Romans 5:14)
Who was in need of redemption?	(Ruth 3:9)	(Titus 2:13-14)
Which kinsman (close relative) was willing and able to redeem?	(Ruth 3:13)	(Galatians 3:13-14)
Which kinsman (close relative) was willing but NOT able to redeem?	(Ruth 3:12; 4:6)	(Psalm 49:7)
Who was redeemed and became a bride?	(Ruth 4:13)	(2 Corinthians 11:2)

D **My Kinsman-Redeemer.** When Boaz redeemed Ruth, he paid a large sum of money to buy the land and the right to marry her. When Christ redeemed you, how did He make the payment?

_____

Write a prayer of thanksgiving to God for His payment for you.

_____
_____
_____

18

E **The "Great" Big Plan.** God had big plans for Ruth and Boaz. They were part of the family from which the Messiah would come. Read Matthew 1:1-17 and fill in the missing people in Jesus' genealogy.

(Stars: 1, 2, 3, 4, 5 Perez, 6 Hezron, 7 Ram, 8 Amminadab, 9 Nahshon, 10, 11, 12, 13, 14, Jesus Christ)

F **God's Providence.** Describe one way you see God's providence at work in your life.

_____
_____
_____

75

G **Defining Loyalty.** Use your dictionary and glossary to write a definition of **loyalty**. Then finish the acrostic using each letter to begin a word or phrase that describes **loyalty**. One has already been done for you.

Loyalty means _____

_____

L _____

O _____

You do not betray a trust.

A _____

L _____

T _____

Y _____

HI!

H **You . . . Whooo?** Read the verses and write to whom God wants you to be loyal. Then think of others and write their names in the empty boxes.

Whooo . . . whooom are you loyal to?

Ephesians 6:2

Proverbs 17:17

Hebrews 10:25

1 Kings 8:61

Matthew 22:37-39

My Loyalty Tree

76

Overview of the United Kingdom   19

A Israel Demands a King.
Israel seemed to be going in the wrong direction when they asked God for a king. Read the verses in 1 Samuel 8. Then fill in the blanks to complete the statements.

Israel had rejected the _Lord_ . (v.7)

Israel wanted a king like the other _nations_ . (v.5)

Israel had forsaken the Lord to serve other _gods_ . (v.8)

God told Samuel to _warn_ Israel. (v.9)

B God's Wise Warnings.
God warned Israel what would happen if He should give them a king. Read 1 Samuel 8:11-17. On the signs list the things a human king would do to Israel. Then answer the question below.

WARNING! sons for head men

WARNING! no of the grain and cattle

WARNING! cooks and perfumers

WARNING! make ishad servants to be slaves

WARNING! appoint captain

WARNING! not cry for king not get what they need

Why was it not God's best for Israel to have a human king?
a selfish king

We Three Kings. Three kings ruled during the United Kingdom period in Israel's history. Do you know who was the wisest? The tallest? The most tender to God? Use the verses to fill in the chart and answer the questions about them. Where no verses are listed, you will need to look in your glossary under the king's name for your answers. Some answers have already been filled in for you.

The United Kingdom

	SAUL	DAVID	SOLOMON
Anointed By?	Samuel (1 Samuel 10:1)	Samuel (1 Samuel 16:13)	Zadok (1 Kings 1:39)
Length of Reign?	40 years (Acts 13:21)	40 years (2 Samuel 5:4)	40 Years
Key Attribute?	he was the tallest (1 Samuel 9:2)	he was tender (Acts 13:22)	he was wisdom (1 Kings 4:30-31)
From What Tribe?	Benjamin (1 Samuel 9:21)	Juda (2 Samuel 2:4)	Juda (Hint: Solomon was David's son.)
Writings?	none	Psalms	Proverbs
Major Role?	Began the establishment of the Kingdom Period	Established the kingdom and expanded Israel's land	built temple (1 Kings 6:1)

19

D

Narrowing the Options. Do you remember the covenant God made with Abraham? God said He would bless Abraham with a land, a nation and a seed, which meant a very special descendant in whom all the nations of the world would be blessed. Read the verses and circle the sons who would be in the line of God's special seed.

Abraham had two sons:	Ishmael and Isaac	(Genesis 17:19)
Isaac had two sons:	Esau and Jacob	(Genesis 28:3-4)
Jacob had twelve sons:	Issachar; Naphtali; Dan; Gad; Asher; Reuben; Judah; Simeon; Levi; Benjamin; Zebulun; and Joseph	(Genesis 49:10)

Which of the three kings received the promise of the seed in his line? Read 2 Samuel 7:16-17 and write his name on the line below.

_____

E

A "Prophetic" Promise. Austin and Katie are going around in circles trying to find the three things God promised to King David. Read 2 Samuel 7:16-17 and write the three things which will continue forever. Cross off every second and third letters and write the name given to God's promise with David. Help Katie answer Austin's question.

God's promise with David is sometimes called the _____

Start Here

How is God's covenant with David like a circle?

F **Meet Jim and Joanie Discontent.** Have you ever heard yourself make comments similar to the ones Jim and Joanie have made below? Circle the three that are most similar to ones you say at home. In the margin beside each, write a better statement that shows a more contented attitude. Then answer the questions.

- Dad, why do I have to wash the dishes every night?
- Yuk! I hate eggs for breakfast. I don't see why Mom has to make them all the time.
- I don't really want to go to the party if I don't have a new outfit to wear. After all, my friend has a new outfit.
- If I were the only child in this family I'd have the CD player to myself.
- I can't believe we have to go to church again tonight. I'll miss my favorite T.V. program.
- I wish I had Mrs. Olsen for my teacher. My teacher gives too much homework.
- I don't see why we have to go to bed at 9:00. That's a dumb rule.
- I'll never ride bikes with the Smith kids anymore. They're no fun!

Home of Jim and Joanie Discontent

Which one of the above comments was most like Israel's attitude when they wanted a human king. Why?

_____
_____
_____

G **God's WRITE Provisions and Promises.** Read 1 Timothy 6:6-8 and Hebrews 13:5 and write a note to Jim and Joanie telling them what God says about contentment.

Dear Jim and Joanie,
_____
_____
_____

80

Samuel: Sensitivity to God

A

Standing in Samuel's Place. Can you imagine how it felt at a very young age to be taken to live with a stranger? That's just what happened to Samuel. Pretend you are Samuel looking back at your dedication experience. Were you sad or happy? Review the story in 1 Samuel 1:24-27. Write about how you felt when your mother left you at the Temple.

B

Searchin' for Facts. Dr. Diggit and Dusty are searching for answers to their questions about Samuel's unusual birth and life. Read the verses in 1 Samuel and answer the questions. Connect the letters that spell the answers to the questions. The words can go in all directions and twist around. (The first one has been done for you.) Then answer the questions below.

1. Who was Samuel's mother? (1:20) _____

2. Who was Samuel's father? (1:21-22) _____

3. Where was Samuel born? (1:19) _____

4. Under which priest did Samuel serve? (3:1) _____

5. What vow did Samuel's mother make to God before his birth? (1:11)

    Hint: no haircut _____

6. Who granted Samuel's mother her desire to have a son? (1:27)

_____

7. When did Samuel begin serving God? (2:18) _____

8. From which tribe was Samuel? (1 Chronicles 6:1, 25-28)

_____

9. How did Hannah know God listened to her request? _____

_____

10. How do you know when God listens to you? _____

_____

C

"Here, Hear!" Review the story of Samuel's call in 1 Samuel 3:1-18. Unscramble the words and write them in the appropriate blanks to complete the statements. In the circles, number the events in the order they happened.

Word Bank
SUMLEA
RODL
OIVNIS
ABCNTEAELR
TVIYGEENHR
GANIA
HDRTI
EKPAS
LEI

◯ The Lord called _____.
◯ The Lord called _____.
◯ The _____ came and stood by Samuel.
◯ The Lord sent Samuel a _____.
◯ Eli asked Samuel to tell him _____.
◯ Samuel was lying down in the _____.
◯ Eli told Samuel to say, "_____ Lord, . . ."
◯ The Lord called Samuel a _____ time.
◯ Samuel said to _____, "Here I am."

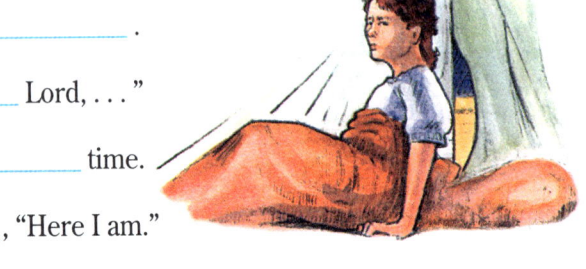

Why didn't Samuel recognize the Lord's voice the first time? Read 1 Samuel 3:7 and John 10:27 to write an answer to the question.

_____

D

Wearing Three Hats. Did you know God called Samuel to serve in three positions? Read the verses and write his three jobs inside the headpieces. (You will only need to fill in two letters for one.) Then answer the question.

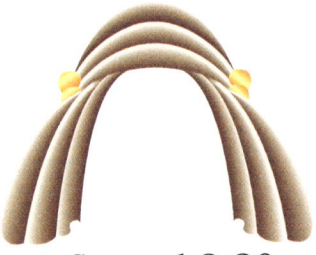

1 Samuel 3:20 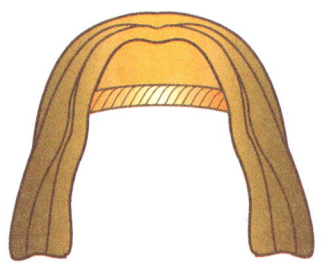   1 Samuel 7:15    1 Samuel 2:18
                                       P__ie__t

How did Israel know that Samuel was a true prophet of the Lord? Compare Deuteronomy 18:21-22 and 1 Samuel 3:16-20 to find the answer to the question.

_____
_____

20

E **Call It . . . I-N-T-E-R-F-E-R-E-N-C-E.** Did you know being sensitive to God includes being attentive to God's Word and acting on what He says? Read the interpretation of the "Parable of the Sower" in Matthew 13:18-23 and write under each picture the hindrances that keep you from responding when God speaks to you.

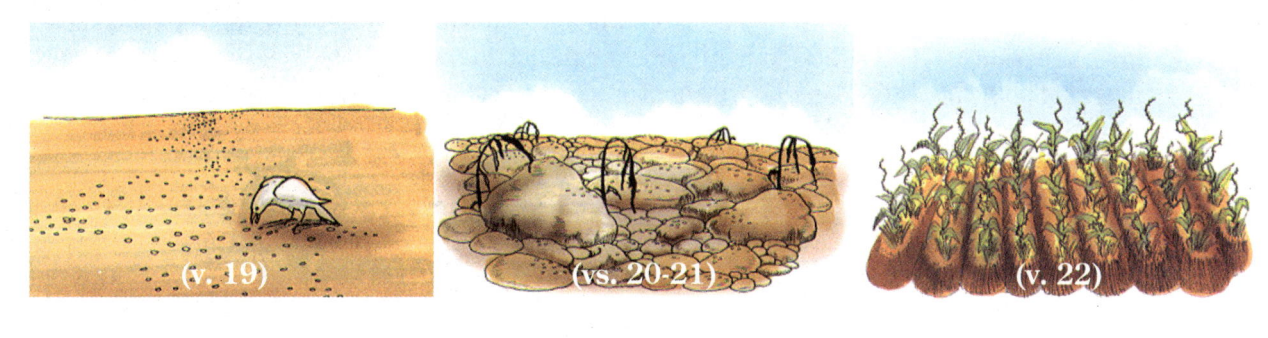

(v. 19)   (vs. 20-21)   (v. 22)

_____   _____   _____

F **Big Ears.** Are your ears big enough? How much time do you spend listening to God each week as opposed to doing other things? Let's compare the two. There are 168 hours every week; you are awake approximately 100 hours of them. In the first column, write the number of hours you spend in activities listening to God. Next to each item in column two list the number of hours you spend doing other things. Then answer the question.

The Hours I Listen To God In . . .	The Hours I Spend . . .
_____ Bible study	_____ Being with friends
_____ Devotions and prayer	_____ Eating
_____ Sunday School	_____ Watching T.V.
_____ A church service	_____ Listening to C.D.'s
_____ Memorizing Scripture	_____ Studying in school
_____ Total Hours	_____ Total Hours

How could you change your present schedule to allow more time to listen to God?

_____

_____

G   **This Is Your Life, Samuel.** When Samuel gave his speech, he shared the things that were important to him. He also showed his character. Using what you have learned about Samuel and reading what Samuel says about himself in the verses below, design a badge that identifies two characteristics. The first characteristic, "Sensitive To God," has already been written in for you. Write the verse that best fits it on the line beside it. Then write another characteristic and the appropriate verse in the other blank. Illustrate both characteristics with a symbol or some event in Samuel's life. Be ready to give reasons for your choices.

1 Samuel 12:1-4; 1 Samuel 12:14-15
1 Samuel 12:16-18; 1 Samuel 12:19-22

MY NAME IS SAMUEL

Characteristic	Reference	Characteristic	Reference
Sensitive to God	_____	_____	_____

What characteristic about Samuel do you most admire and why? List something you might do to reflect that same characteristic.

_____
_____
_____

Saul: Pride and Disobedience

21

A

Help Wanted! Can you believe it? Years before Israel had a king, God told Moses Israel would someday have a king and even listed some of the qualifications for the job. Pretend you are the one hiring a king. Read Deuteronomy 17:14-20. Then use the qualifications listed in the verses to complete the newspaper want ad for a king.

The Israel Times

Want Ads Section — 1050 B.C.

Help Wanted: A King to serve in Israel.
He must... _____

B

The First Applicant. If Saul were applying for the job as king today, what information would be on his job application? Read the verses in 1 Samuel and fill out the application.

Job Application For King

Applicant's Name: (9:2) _____

Tribe: (9:21) _____   City Address: (10:26) _____

Family Background: (9:1, 21)

Father: _____   Family Status: _____   Physical Condition: (9:2) _____

Qualifications: (Check the qualities that describe Saul.)

___ Humble (9:21; 10:21-22)   Why? _____

___ Leadership (11:11-15)   Why? _____

___ Forgiving (10:27)   Why? _____

___ Religious (15:24-25)   Why? _____

Have you ever been fired? (15:26) Yes. ___ No. ___ If yes, explain. _____

85

C **Checking Up on Saul.** Did you know that much of the original Hebrew language was written without vowels? Help Austin and Katie add vowels to the words to find all the things God instructed Saul to destroy. Then read 1 Samuel 15:7-9 and put a check over each word that shows when Saul obeyed the instruction. (Be careful with the checks!)

c t t l & s h p

n r s n g   c h l d r n

n f n t s

c m l s & d n k y s

m n & w m n

_____ & _____

_____

_____

_____ & _____

_____ & _____

Using the above circled letters, complete the sentence below. Then use your glossary to write a definition of Saul's sin.

Saul had the sin of _____ , which means _____ .

D **A Proud Heart.** Read the verses and answer the questions.

How did King Saul show he had a proud heart? (1 Samuel 15:7-12)

_____

What does God say about pride? (1 John 2:16)

_____

What is the opposite of pride? (James 4:6)

_____

When are you most tempted to have a proud heart?

_____

_____

21

E **Abominable Abominations.** When God tried to make a point of something being really bad, He sometimes used the word **abomination** to describe it. Use your glossary to complete the definition of **abomination**. Then read Deuteronomy 18:9-14 and make a list of the things that are abominable to the Lord.

If the word **abomination** means _____ ,

then the word **abominable** describes something that is _____ .

**WARNING!   WARNING!
THE ABOMINABLE THINGS!**

_____
_____
_____
_____
_____
_____
_____

F **The Consequences.** The abominable things were so awful to God that He pronounced serious judgment on those who took part in them. Read the verses to answer the questions.

Why doesn't God want us to get involved in abominable things? (Leviticus 19:31)

_____
_____

What were the Old Testament consequences of someone who became involved in the abominable things?

(Leviticus 20:27) _____
_____

How can Romans 8:5-6 help you avoid getting caught up in abominable things?

_____
_____

G **Identifying Proud People.** Dr. Diggit is trying to help Austin and Katie identify the proud people in Scripture. Read the verses and check the quality the character in the passage reflects. Give a reason for your choice.

	Pride	Humility
John 3:27-30	☐	☐

Reason: _____

| **2 Chronicles 26:14-16** | ☐ | ☐ |

Reason: _____

| **Genesis 32:9-12** | ☐ | ☐ |

Reason: _____

| **Matthew 11:25-30** | ☐ | ☐ |

Reason: _____

| **1 Kings 1:5** | ☐ | ☐ |

Reason: _____

H **Finding Flaws.** Find flaws in the thinking of each of the students below. Read each student's comment carefully. Then read the following verses: 1 John 2:16; Proverbs 16:18; and Proverbs 29:23. Write the matching reference on the blanks inside the speech balloons.

If I tell my friends at school how my play won the soccer game on Saturday, then surely I'll be picked first for a team today.

Everybody's going to love me in my new dress. God wants me to feel good about myself.

I've got it made! Nothing can keep me from winning the spelling bee now. I don't even have to study.

Choose one dialogue to rewrite, demonstrating a humble response.

_____

_____

David: Confidence in God

22

A

Tuning In... The Harp Player. Dr. Diggit is trying to clear up Austin and Katie's confusion. They have been reading 1 Samuel 16:18 in several Bible versions. Read this Scripture in your Bible and circle the eight descriptions of David. Draw lines from each of these phrases to other phrases which mean the same thing.

- son of Jesse
- of Bethlehem
- knows how to play the harp
- a mighty valiant man
- a brave man
- prudent in matters
- a comely person
- cunning in playing
- a warrior
- speaks well
- a valiant man
- a fine looking man
- the Bethlehemite
- a man of war
- prudent in speech
- a handsome man
- plays skillfully
- skillful in playing
- a handsome person
- a mighty man of valor
- a skilled musician
- eloquent
- an attractive person
- the Lord is with him

B

Living in Harmony with God. David seemed to have a lot of good qualities, but what was it about David that caused God to choose him as the second king of Israel? Use the musical code to find how David lived in harmony with God according to Acts 13:22.

| A | D | E | F | G | H | I | L | M | N | O | R | S | T | W |

David lived in harmony with God because he was a…

MAN AFTER GOD'S OWN HEART AND HE DID GOD'S WILL.

GIANT GO-OPOLY

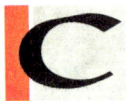

Bedrock Character Qualities
- Faith in God
- Concern for God
- Courage
- Honesty
- Joyfulness

Rock Pile #1
Rock Pile #2
Rock Pile #3
Rock Pile #4
Rock Pile #5

Board spaces (clockwise from Go):
- Go.
- Take a rock from Pile #5.
- David advances toward Goliath. **Advance 2** I Samuel 17:48
- Goliath curses David. **Retreat 1** I Samuel 17:43
- Take a rock from Pile #4.
- Goliath despises David. **Retreat 2** I Samuel 17:42
- Saul gives David too much armor. **Retreat 1** I Samuel 17:38-39
- Take a rock from Pile #3.
- Saul thinks David is too young. **Retreat 3** I Samuel 17:33
- Eliab rebukes David. **Retreat 1** I Samuel 17:28
- Take a rock from Pile #2.
- Saul announces a reward. **Advance 1** I Samuel 17:25
- Israel runs away from Goliath. **Retreat 2** I Samuel 17:24
- Take a rock from Pile #1.
- Saul is fearful. **Retreat 2** I Samuel 17:11

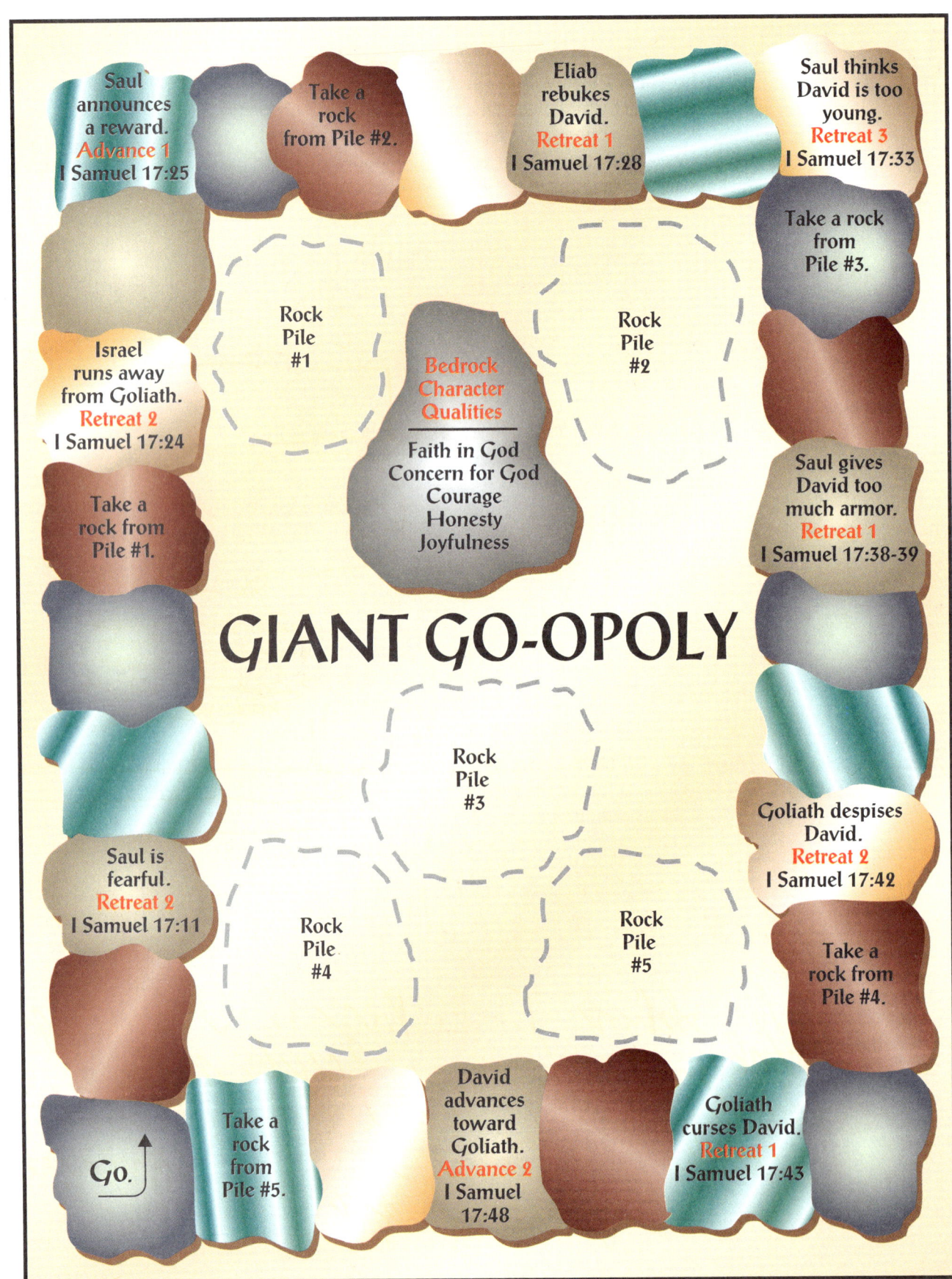

22

D **The Shepherd's Psalm.** How would you like to hide in caves and be hunted by your enemies? That was the way David lived. But it didn't keep him from giving his heart to God. The 23rd Psalm will give you an idea of how David chose to trust God completely even in the midst of bad circumstances. Listen while your teacher gives you directions.

The 23rd Psalm

The Lord is my Shepherd; I shall not want.

He makes me to lie down in green pastures;
He leads me beside the still waters.

He restores my soul; He leads me in the paths
of righteousness for His name's sake.

Yea, though I walk through the valley
of the shadow of death, I will fear no evil;
For You are with Me; Your rod and Your staff,
they comfort me.

You prepare a table before me
in the presence of my enemies;
You anoint my head with oil;
My cup runs over.

Surely goodness and mercy shall follow me
all the days of my life; and I will dwell
in the house of the Lord forever.

E **Responding to My Shepherd.** David shared his feelings and beliefs about God through his songs. Think about a time in your life when God showed Himself to you as your Shepherd. To write your own psalm (song) fill in your beliefs and feelings about God. Be ready to share it and to give reasons for your choices.

The Lord is my _Savior_; I shall not _beg_. He makes me to _do good_; He _takes care of me_ and He _guides me_. Yea, though I _when the devil is on (tempting)_ I will not _fear the devil_. For You are _God_. Your _rock_ and _stone_ help me because they _save me_. Surely _peace and comfort_ will follow me all my days.

91

F **Missing Heart Parts.** Austin and Katie have looked everywhere for the questions to their assignments, but they can only find the answers. Read the verses and write the questions on the lines that correspond to the "Answers" on the right.

Questions	Answers
1. Matthew 5:8 _____ ?	1. the pure in heart
2. Matthew 15:19 _____ ?	2. evil thoughts, murderers, thefts and false witnesses
3. Matthew 15:18 _____ ?	3. the things that come from the mouth
4. Jeremiah 17:9 _____ ?	4. the heart
5. 1 Samuel 16:7 _____ ?	5. God looks on the heart.
6. 1 Chronicles 28:9 _____ ?	6. The Lord searches all hearts.

G **Heart Matters.** What is in your heart matters to God. To find out about your heart attitude, check the appropriate boxes.

Always	Sometimes	Never	
☐	☐	☐	I read my Bible every day.
☐	☐	☐	I pray daily for others' needs.
☐	☐	☐	I feel bad when others hurt.
☐	☐	☐	I treat my parents with respect.
☐	☐	☐	I consistently obey my teacher.
☐	☐	☐	I speak kindly to my classmates.
☐	☐	☐	I am honest when I give answers.
☐	☐	☐	I seek God's direction.

David: Sin and Consequences

23

A **Mixed-Up Disorder.** Read 2 Samuel 11 and number in order the things David did when he sinned.

- 8 made Uriah drunk
- 5 sent for Bathsheba
- 3 noticed Bathsheba's beauty
- 2 walked on his roof
- 12 married Bathsheba
- 10 plotted Uriah's death
- 7 told Uriah to go home
- 1 stayed home from war
- 6 committed immorality
- 11 put Uriah in front
- 4 asked who Bathsheba was
- 9 wrote letter to Joab

B **Broken Commandments.** David broke more than just one of God's Ten Commandments. Put a check by the number of each commandment he broke. Then answer Dr. Diggit's question by writing the number of the commandments in the blanks.

1. You shall have no other gods before Me.
2. You shall not make for yourself a carved image....
3. You shall not take the name of the Lord your God in vain....
4. Remember the Sabbath day to keep it holy.
5. Honor your father and your mother....
6. You shall not murder.
7. You shall not commit adultery.
8. You shall not steal.
9. You shall not bear false witness (lie)....
10. You shall not covet your neighbor's house; you shall not covet your neighbor's wife....

Logically speaking, which commands did David break first __1__, second __6__, third __7__, and fourth __10__?

93

C Shaping Up.

What choices did David make that helped get him back in shape after he sinned? Answer the questions by writing the correct word in the blank. Then use the words to complete a statement in the box that tells what David chose to do and what God did.

What word is **only** in the…

1. ○, □ and △? _forgave_
2. ○? _confessed_
3. △, □ and □? ~~God~~ _him_
4. □? _sins_
5. △ and ○? _of_
6. □ and ○? _he_
7. △? _David_
8. □ and △? _and_
9. □? _convicted_
10. ○, △, □ and □? _God_
11. △ and □? _was_
12. ○ and □? _his_

David _____ .

D The Three C's.

Read the verses in 2 Samuel and follow the directions.

Write the words Nathan said to David that brought **conviction**.

_____ (12:1-7)

Write what David said when he made his **confession** of sin.

_____ (12:13)

List some of the **consequences** God said David would suffer.

_____
_____ (12:11,14)

23

E
Gone Forever. Have you ever felt guilty even after you've asked God to forgive you? Read the verses and draw a picture in each box illustrating what the Bible says God's forgiveness of sin is really like.

Psalm 103:12

Jeremiah 31:34

Isaiah 1:18

F
Mercy, Mercy and More Mercy. Wow! God just keeps on showing more and more mercy to us. Read the verses and complete one truth about God's mercy in the heart diagram. Then include the truth in a prayer of thanksgiving to God for His mercy.

God's mercy is. . .

Titus 3:5   Daniel 9:9   Micah 7:18

Dear Lord,

I want to thank You for Your great mercy because it...

G **Please Answer My Question.** Dr. Diggit is answering questions about God's mercy. Read the verses and choose the one that best fits each question. In the speech balloons write what Dr. Diggit would have to say in order to give the Biblical answer. (Hebrews 4:16; Daniel 9:9; Psalm 51:7; 1 Chronicles 16:34)

- How can I know God will have mercy on me even after I've sinned? _____ Reference
- How can I be sure I can count on God's mercy in the future as I have in the past? _____ Reference
- What is the first step in finding mercy with God? _____ Reference

H **Clothe Yourself with Mercy.** Did you know that by showing mercy to others you are reflecting God's attribute of mercy? In Colossians 3:12 the Apostle Paul encouraged Christians to "... put on mercy..." much the same way as you put on your clothes. Read the following situations. Write at least one way you might show mercy in each situation.

My dad lost his job and my mother had to go to work. To show mercy to my mother I would…
_____

My little brother received a bad grade in math. To show mercy to my brother I would…
_____

A friend down the street does not know Jesus as Savior. To show mercy to my friend I would…
_____

Absalom: Rebellion

24

A. Root Problems.
Read the verses in 2 Samuel. Fill in the words that best complete Absalom's story. Then copy the words in the puzzle below to find the root of Absalom's problem.

David's sin brought great consequences and grief to his household. The prophet Nathan said the _sword_ (12:10) would never depart from David's house, which meant that death would come to his own family. One of David's sons, Absalom, _hated_ (13:22) his _brother_ Amnon (13:26) for defiling his _sister_ (13:22) Tamar. Absalom said to his men, "_kill_ (13:28) my brother." Absalom _fled_ (13:38) to Geshur. Later Absalom and his spies plotted to have the people of _Israel_ (15:10) proclaim him king. He staged a fierce battle against his father's forces. Twenty _thousand_ (18:7) men died in the slaughter. Absalom caught his long hair in the low branches of a tree and was killed by one of David's men. King David was deeply grieved to hear his _son_ (18:33) Absalom had died.

B. Look It Up.
Use your glossary to write the meaning of REBELLION below Absalom's picture.

Rebellion: an act of opposition or an uprising those in authority

1. s w o r d
2. h a t e d
3. b r o t h e r
4. s i s t e r
5. k i l l
6. f l e d
7. i s r a e l
8. t h o u s a n d
9. s o n

C The Pattern of Rebellion. Draw a line from the references in 2 Samuel to the events they describe. Then identify the trait of rebellion which fits.

Rebellion

conspiring, unforgiving, disloyalty, hate, overly-ambitious

References / Events

13:22 — Absalom tried to get the men of Israel to follow him instead of his father the king. — *disloyalty*

15:6 — Absalom instructed Israel to proclaim him king. — *overly-ambitious*

13:28 — Absalom despised his brother. — *hate*

15:12 — Absalom never forgot the evil his brother did and eventually had him killed. — *unforgiving*

15:10 — Absalom's evil plans gained strength. — *conspiring*

D Breaking the Pattern. Think of an area in your life where you need to be submissive and obedient. Are you ever tempted to rebel? Read the Scriptures and summarize three steps in breaking the pattern of rebellion.

Proverbs 3:5

Philippians 4:8

Psalm 119:11

24

E **The Ultimate Rebel: Satan.** Satan made some bold claims about what he would do and be like. Read Isaiah 14:13-15 and write his five "I will" statements. Then answer the question.

- I WILL. . . _____
- I WILL. . . _____
- I WILL. . . _____
- I WILL. . . _____
- I WILL. . . _____

How was Absalom's attitude like Satan's "I will" attitude?

_____
_____

F **My "I Will."** Did you know that you make "I will" statements too? Read the "I Will" statements around the doubled fist and circle the ones with which you have the most problem. Then write in one that isn't listed.

"I will watch T.V. before I do my homework."

"I will talk on the phone all evening if I want to."

"I will play the position I want on the team, or I won't play at all."

"I will eat as much candy as I want."

"When someone hurts me, I will look for a chance to get even with him."

"I will *destroy the ministry of ?*"

When you say, "I will . . . ," you are making a choice. Write an "I will" statement that illustrates how you have chosen to follow God's will.

_____
_____
_____

G **Well Versed.** How do you think it made David feel to have one of his own sons, Absalom, chasing after him? Read Psalm 3. Write the verse references that show what David chose to believe about God even when he ran from his rebellious son.

God is my protection. _____

God will bless His people. _____

God will help me not to be fearful. _____

God knows my enemies are increasing. _____

God will hear me and answer my prayer. _____

God is the One who will deliver me from enemies. _____

God will help though my enemies are saying He won't. _____

H **Good Advice.** Some of Austin and Katie's friends have written "Dear Gabby" for advice. Write an answer back and include some of the truths about God from Psalm 3.

Dear Gabby,
Some boys in my school have a gang. Last Saturday night they decided to toss some rocks through the windows at our school. I didn't want to go along, but I was afraid not to. I don't want them to think I'm chicken.

Signed,
Confused

Dear Gabby,
There's this boy on my bus who always picks on me. He calls me names like "shorty" and "stupid." Yesterday he tripped me as I got on the bus. I'm afraid to even go to school anymore. What can I do? I've never done anything to him!

Signed,
Scared

Solomon: Wisdom

25

A

Reasoning the Real Reasons. What was the real reason Solomon asked God for wisdom? Read 1 Kings 3:7-9 and circle the prayer that best describes the reason. Fill in the speech balloon with the exact words of his prayer to God. Then answer the questions.

Lord, if I were the wisest person in the world, I would build the Temple for You so that all Israel could worship You.

Lord, I need Your wisdom more than anything else. Without it I will not know how to judge Your people.

Lord, if You will give me wisdom, then Israel will trust me and obey You more when I give them Your instructions.

Lord, I desire to have wisdom so that the people will honor me as the king You have chosen.

Even though Solomon was 20 years old, he said he felt like a "little child." (1 Kings 3:7) What did this statement show about his heart attitude?

Why was Solomon's decision to ask for wisdom rather than riches and a long life a wise choice? (Proverbs 4:7)

B

Are You Getting It? Austin and Katie started a list of things they need to do to "Get wisdom!" Read the verses and write two things you can choose to do to "get wisdom."

To "get wisdom" you must choose to...

1. _____ (Proverbs 3:1)
2. _____ (James 1:5-6)

101

C **A Real Puzzler???** Solomon's wisdom helped him figure out a complicated puzzle. Read the verses in 1 Kings 3 and work the puzzle.

Two **1 ⤵** _____ (v. 16) came to Solomon with a problem. They both gave **2 ⤵** _____ (v. 17) to **3 ⤴** _____ (v. 18) in the same **4 ⤵** _____ (v. 18). They argued before King **5 ⤴** ____ about whose son had **6 ⤴** _____ (v. 22). King Solomon told the women he would **7 ⤵** ____ (v. 25) the living **8 ⤴** _____ (v. 25) in half and give a part to **9 ⤴** _____ (v. 25). When the **10 ⤴** _____ (v. 26) woman was willing to give the child up to the **11 ⤵** _____ (v. 26) woman in order to save the child from the **12 ⤴** _____ (v. 24), then Solomon gave the child to the first **13 ⤴** _____ (v. 27). Then **14 ⤵** _____ (v. 28) saw that God had given King **15 ⤵** _____ (v. 28) the ability to rule with **16 ⤴** _____ (v. 28).

D **Understanding Wisdom.** Use your glossary to write the definition of wisdom. Then answer the question.

_____

_____

Suppose you spent the night with your best friend, and the next day that friend tried to persuade you to go to a movie of which you knew your parents would not approve. What would you choose to do? Using your past experience and knowledge of right and wrong, describe the wisest choice you could make and the reasons for your choice.

_____

_____

_____

25

E **Foolhearted King Solomon.** How could such a wise king become so foolish? Where did he go wrong? To find the answer, read the verses. Circle the one that Solomon needed to apply but didn't. Summarize why you chose it.

Proverbs 14:24	Proverbs 13:20	Proverbs 14:1

F **Foolproof and Wise.** Dr. Diggit has been searching for the truth again, and he has just made a great find. Read the verses from Proverbs and fill in the chart to find out how differently wise and foolish people think and act. On the rocks finish the definitions of "foolish" and "wise" people.

Reference	Foolish People	Wise People
1:5a, 7b		
10:1		
12:15		
14:6		
15:2		
29:11		

THE FOOLISH PERSON IS SOMEONE WHO...

BUT, THE WISE PERSON IS SOMEONE WHO...

103

G **A Wise Foundation.** Matthew 7:24-27 tells how two builders built their houses. Compare the wise and foolish man, and write a statement under the foundation of each that tells the difference. Then answer Dusty's question.

I wonder how a wise man becomes so wise . . . ?

A wise man becomes wise by
_____
_____
_____
_____
_____
_____
_____

_____
_____

H **Wise Up!** Austin and Katie's friends need some wisdom. Read the life situation. Then choose the reference that would most help each friend apply God's wisdom. (Proverbs 19:20; Proverbs 22:10; and Proverbs 22:1).

Life Situation #1
Kelly wanted to win the class reading contest. Mrs. Cambell, her teacher, said the first place winner would receive a new book of his or her choice from the book club catalog. Kelly had already made her choice if she won. Her friends told her to record more books than she had really read and then quickly read them after the contest. Kelly thought about it. If she did that, she would win the book she wanted for sure.

Which Bible truth should be applied? _____

Life Situation #2
Ben was glad when he found out Neal had been put on his soccer team. Ben's parents did not want him to become too friendly with Neal because Neal always seemed to be getting into trouble. Although Neal sometimes made fun of Ben for going to church so much, Ben still liked to be around Neal and wanted to become better friends. Ben thought about it. If he wanted to be buddies with Neal, then why not?

Which Bible truth should be applied? _____

Solomon: Talents and Treasures Given to God

26

A
Using Treasures and Talents. Solomon only asked God for wisdom, but God also gave him treasures as well. Read 2 Chronicles 1:11-15 and write the talents and treasures with which God blessed Solomon on the gold pieces surrounding the treasure chest. Then answer the question.

How did Solomon use his treasures for the Lord? Why? (2 Chronicles 2:1)

___

B
Rating Your Talents and Treasures. Have you ever thought about how you use your talents and treasures for God? On a scale of one to five, circle the number you think you deserve.

	NEVER	Hardly Ever	SOMETIMES	Most of the Time	Always
1. I give part of my allowance to the church.	1	2	3	4	5
2. I spend time telling others about God.	1	2	3	4	5
3. I help missionaries by praying and giving.	1	2	3	4	5
4. I use the gift God has given me to encourage my friends at church.	1	2	3	4	5
5. I use whatever talents God has given me to help people who are needy.	1	2	3	4	5

C **Solomon Builds the Temple.** Austin and Katie are trying to figure out what goes where in the Temple. Read the verses in 2 Chronicles 4-5, and label the Temple areas and furniture in the diagram below.

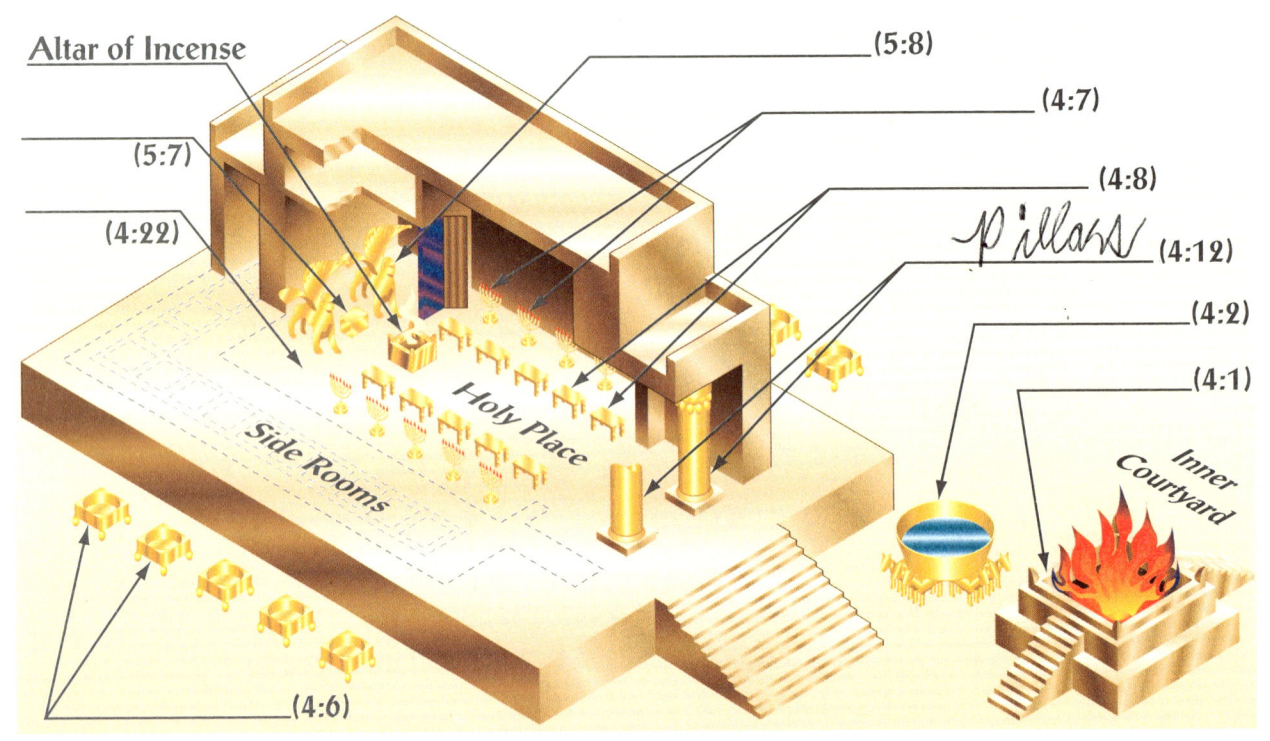

Altar of Incense
(5:8)
(5:7)
(4:7)
(4:22)
(4:8)
pillars (4:12)
(4:2)
(4:1)
Side Rooms
Holy Place
Inner Courtyard
(4:6)

D **Only the Best.** Solomon spared no costs when he built a house for God. Read 2 Chronicles 3:5-9, 14-17. Circle the decorations he used in the Temple. Then answer the question.

S	V	M	I	B	U	R	E	H	C	D	E	V	R	A	C	P	O	N	M
S	E	T	A	N	A	R	G	E	M	O	P	D	D	L	G	E	N	I	P
D	I	E	E	D	A	D	I	N	G	N	A	E	L	O	F	F	I	R	E
L	L	S	S	O	P	Y	E	N	O	T	S	S	U	O	I	C	E	R	P
O	A	Z	N	W	O	R	K	G	L	K	O	P	T	G	G	E	R	U	P
G	Y	P	I	L	L	A	R	S	D	N	A	I	L	S	F	E	G	H	T
E	A	O	A	P	A	L	M	T	R	E	E	D	E	S	I	G	N	S	F
R	R	W	H	M	I	R	C	E	L	P	R	U	P	E	U	L	B	I	N
U	N	T	C	S	O	N	V	E	I	L	N	E	N	I	L	E	N	I	F
P	T	P	O	M	C	H	C	U	R	T	A	I	N	S	D	L	O	G	I

Why did Solomon work hard to make the Temple a place of beauty? (2:5)

26

E

Generous Givers. Compare 1 Kings 10:13 and Ephesians 3:20 to answer the question.

How does Solomon's generosity to the Queen of Sheba remind you of Christ's generosity to us?

_____
_____
_____
_____

F

Golden Gifts. Have you ever thought of how valuable God's gifts are to us? Read the verses and identify His gifts.

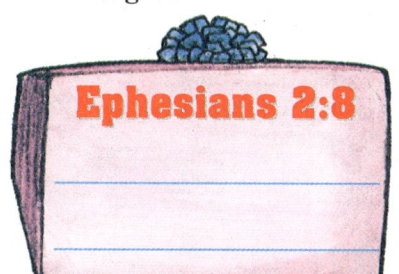

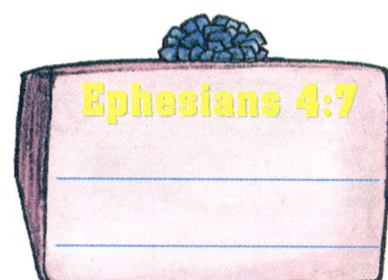

Ephesians 2:8

Romans 3:23

Ephesians 4:7

Romans 1:11

Luke 11:13

In Luke 11:31 the Bible says "a greater than Solomon is here" when it talks about Christ. Read James 1:17 and circle the two phrases that complete the statement. Write two other phrases that complete the statement and describe God's gifts to you.

God's gifts to me are better than Solomon's gifts to the Queen of Sheba because they...

are more expensive.   are perfect.   will make me rich.   are eternal.

_____
_____

G **Living Parables.** Will, Bette and Brad have certain abilities. Look at the pictures and decide what their abilities are. Cross out the picture of the person who has already buried his or her ability. Then underneath each picture, illustrate how each student could use those abilities for God.

"Will's such a good athlete."

"Yes, and a good leader, too!"

"I'm glad Bette won the contest. She's so kind to everyone."

"Brad, would you help me with my math?"

"No, I'm too busy."

H **Living Out the Parable.** Are you choosing to use the abilities God has given to you? Think of one ability God has given to you and write it in the margin. Then read 1 Corinthians 4:2 and complete the commitment statement to show how you can apply the verse in using your ability.

MY COMMITMENT FOR STEWARDSHIP

Since the quality required to be a good servant is _____

and God has given me the ability to _____ ,

then I will use my ability for God by _____

_____ and _____ .

CERTIFICATE

108

Overview of the Divided Kingdom

27

A. Division Decisions.
Rehoboam and Jeroboam had some king-sized problems. Use the verses in 1 Kings 12 and fill in each king's solution. Then answer the question below.

King Rehoboam's Problem

The people wanted Rehoboam to lighten their work, and they told the king they would serve him if he would do it. If Rehoboam made a wise decision, then he would help to keep peace in Israel. What did he do?

King Rehoboam's Division Decision

He asked the _____ (v.6) for their _____ (v.6), but he _____ (v.8) it. Then he asked the _____ (v. 8) men for their advice. They told him not to _____ (v.15) to the people, so he didn't. Israel divided afterward.

King Jeroboam's Problem

If the people in the Northern Kingdom decided to travel back to Jerusalem to offer sacrifices, then they might decide to kill Jeroboam and give their support once again to Rehoboam. What did he do?

King Jeroboam's Division Decision

He asked _____ (v.28) and made two _____ (v.28) out of _____ (v. 28). He set them up in _____ and _____ (v. 29) and the people _____ (v.30) them. Jeroboam had created another place to worship.

What was the consequence of each man's decision?

_____

B. Dividing the Code.
Work the math problems. Then use the answers and the code to find the new names of the Northern and Southern Kingdoms.

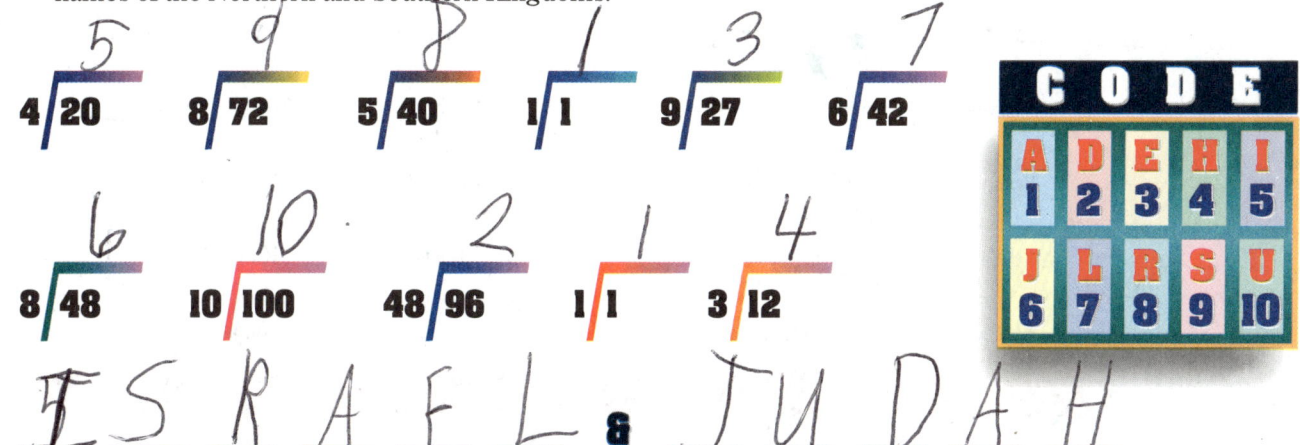

5 9 8 1 3 7
4/20 8/72 5/40 1/1 9/27 6/42

CODE
A	D	E	H	I
1	2	3	4	5
J	L	R	S	U
6	7	8	9	10

6 10 2 1 4
8/48 10/100 48/96 1/1 3/12

I S R A E L & J U D A H

The Good and the Bad. Dr. Diggit has been trying to identify the kings who ruled in both Israel and Judah. Help him complete the chart by writing the name of the king or the characteristics of good or evil in the blanks.

Kings of Israel (N. Kingdom)			Kings of Judah (S. Kingdom)		
Name	Reference	Character	Name	Reference	Character
	1 Kings 13:33	Evil		2 Chronicles 10:18-19	Evil
Nadab	1 Kings 15:25-26		Abijam	1 Kings 15:1-3	Evil
Baasha	1 Kings 16:7	Evil		1 Kings 15:11	Good
Elah	1 Kings 16:13		Jehoshaphat	1 Kings 22:42-43	
Zimri	1 Kings 16:20	Evil		2 Kings 8:16-18	Evil
Omri	1 Kings 16:25		Ahaziah	2 Kings 8:25-27	
	1 Kings 16:30	Evil	Joash	2 Chronicles 24:2	
Ahaziah	1 Kings 22:51-52		Amaziah	2 Chronicles 25:1-2	
Jehoram	2 Kings 3:1-2	Evil	Azariah	2 Kings 15:1-3	
Jehu	2 Kings 10:29,31		Jotham	2 Chronicles 27:1-2	
Jehoahaz	2 Kings 13:1-2			2 Kings 17:1-2	Evil
Jeroboam II	2 Kings 14:23-24	Evil	Hezekiah	2 Chronicles 29:1-2	
Zechariah	2 Kings 15:8-9		Manasseh	2 Kings 21:1-2	
Shallum	2 Kings 15:15		Amon	2 Kings 21:19-20	Evil
Menahem	2 Kings 15:17-18		Josiah	2 Kings 22:1-2	
Pekahiah	2 Kings 15:23-24	Evil	Jehoahaz	2 Kings 23:31-32	
Pekah	2 Kings 15:27-28		Jehoiakim	2 Kings 23:36-37	Evil
Hoshea	2 Kings 17:1-2		Zedekiah	2 Kings 24:18-19	

Ahab and Elijah: The Fight Between Good and Evil — 28

A **Let's Face It!** King Ahab and Queen Jezebel were wicked. Read the following verses in 1 Kings and list the sins that made them so evil.

- Ahab did evil in the eyes of the Lord (16:30)
- Worshiped Baal (16:31)
- He built a temple for Baal (16:32)
- He made a wooden image (16:33)
- is killing the Lord's profit [prophet] (18:4,13)
- He urged Jezebel against God (21:25-26)

B **Confronting the Facts.** Who was bold enough to confront such a wicked king and queen? Only one prophet — Elijah. Elijah was able to go before them because he knew and believed something about God. To answer the questions, read the verses and unscramble the letters to write two words on the blanks. Then complete the two statements below.

What did Elijah know about God?
(Deuteronomy 11:16-17)
DWSLLOIG
_ _ _ _ _ _ _ _ , _ _ _ _ _ _ _ _

What did Elijah believe about God?
(1 Kings 17:1a)
VGSLOIDE
_ _ _ _ _ _ _ _ _ _ _ _ _ _ _ _

What did Elijah choose to do about what he knew and believed about God?
(1 Kings 17:1)
HFCAAABE
_ _ _ _ _ _ _ _ _ _ _ _ _ _ _ _

What do you know and believe about God that helps you stand against evil people?

I know God is _the creator_.

I believe God is _Good_.

113

God vs. Baal. The prophets of Baal and the prophet of God acted differently. Read 1 Kings 18:25-39. Write **Baal** or **God** on the lines to indicate which of the prophets did the action. Then write the verse where you found the action. Finally, answer the questions.

Hmmm … Baal's prophets outnumbered God's by how many? _____

Prophet of _____   Prophet of _____   Prophet of _____

Verse _____   Verse _____   Verse _____

Prophet of _____   Prophet of _____   Prophet of _____

Verse _____   Verse _____   Verse _____

What two choices did Elijah give the people? (1 Kings 18:21)

Choice #1 _____

Choice #2 _____

What did the people choose to do and why? (1 Kings 18:38-39)

_____

_____

114

28

D **Confusion Says . . . .** Did Elijah really trust God or not? To find Elijah's confusing responses, read the verses from 1 Kings and cross out words so that the statements are correct.

Elijah believed that he was called to be
[God's servant, king]. (1 Kings 18:36)

Elijah wanted God to answer his prayer so that all people would know [God's punishment, God]. (1 Kings 18:37)

Elijah boldly [killed, rebuked] all the prophets of Baal.
(1 Kings 18:40)

Even after God answered Elijah's prayer and allowed him to experience His [chastisement, power] (1 Kings 18:46), Elijah became [fearful, sad] and ran for his life. (1 Kings 19:3)

To encourage Elijah, God had to send [a raven, an angel] to feed him. (1 Kings 19:5)

E **Syl-lo-gis-man-ia.** To find why Elijah's responses seem confusing, read the syllogisms and fill in the logical conclusions.

Premise #1: A righteous person's prayers are effective.

Premise #2: Elijah's prayers were effective.

Conclusion: Therefore, Elijah was a _____
_____ .

Premise #1: We have a sinful nature.

Premise #2: Elijah had a nature like ours.

Conclusion: Therefore, Elijah had a _____
_____ too.

Read James 5:16-18 to see if your conclusions are also backed by Bible truths. ☐ **YES** ☐ **NO**

In what ways are you like Elijah and why is he an example to follow?

_____
_____
_____
_____

115

F **The "Chief Justice" Judges.** What ever happened to King Ahab, anyway? To find how God showed His justice, read the verses in 2 Kings and identify the members of Ahab's family who were judged by death. Draw a line from each name to the picture that best symbolizes God's method of judgment for each.

(9:24) _____

(9:27) _____

(9:30, 33) _____

(10:6-7) _____

(10:19, 25) _____

G **Final Curtain Call.** Not only did God judge the evil family of Ahab in the Old Testament, but He will also bring a future and final judgment on those who have persecuted His people. Read the following verses and check the oval that tells what God's final judgment will be for each of the persons or people groups. (Revelation 16:16; 19:17-21; 20:10-15)

People or Groups	The Sword	Lake of Fire
Kings of the Earth	○	○
Beast	○	○
Mighty Men	○	○
False Prophet	○	○
Horse Rider	○	○
Devil	○	○
People Not in the Book	○	○

Who is the One who will judge with the sword? Why do you think it will be right for Him to show His justice in this way? (Clue: Revelation 19:11-16 will give you the first answer.)

_____

_____

Elisha: Prophet of Miracles and Mercy — 29

A **Who Am I?** Elijah and Elisha worked similar miracles. Compare the verses and read the riddles carefully. Identify the person and circle the phrase in each riddle that helped you make your decision.

Elijah?

I struck the river with my mantle,
And it divided and left its home.
I walked across on Jordan's bed,
But I walked across alone.

Elisha
(2 Kings 2:8, 13-14)

I raised a widow's son to life
By covering him one times three.
The woman looked at me and said,
"You're a man of God, I see."

Elijah
(1 Kings 17:21-22; 2 Kings 4:32-35)

One day I multiplied some food
To provide a widow's need.
I made both oil and flour grow,
So her family she could feed.

Elijah
(1 Kings 17:13-16; 2 Kings 4:3-7)

...or...

Elisha?

Once soldiers came to meet with me
With rebellion on their minds.
To stop the raiders from their plot,
I prayed, "Lord, make them blind."

_____
(2 Kings 1:10; 6:18)

I tried to help some city men;
Their need was rather dire.
I salted water to show God's power,
Instead of calling down fire.

_____
(1 Kings 18:33-38; 2 Kings 2:19-22)

B **Similar . . . But Different.** Elijah and Elisha were similar but their ministries emphasized different truths about God. Let 1 = A, 2 = B and so on to complete what the prophets each illustrated about God.

__ __ __ __ __ __ __ __ __ __ __ __ __ __ __ __ __
5 12 9 10 1 8   23 1 19   1   16 18 15 16 8 5 20 ,

__ __ __ __ __ __ __ __ __ __ __ __ __ __ __ __
15 6   7 15 4 19   10 21 4 7 13 5 14 20   1 14 4 ,

__ __ __ __ __ __ __ __ __ __ __ __ __ __ __ __
5 12 9 19 8 1   15 6   7 15 4 19   13 5 18 3 25 .

117

C **Big Bad Bears.** Can you imagine what it would be like to be mauled by a bear? The youths in Elisha's day must have displeased God a lot to have Him send bears to judge them. Read through the verses and circle the one that you think best describes the sin the youths committed. Explain why you chose the verse. List the sins or commands you just read about with which both young and old people sometimes have trouble.

Why? _People mock each other._

Sins or Commands? _Mocking people and respect._

1 Thessalonians 5:12-13
Leviticus 19:32
(Proverbs 19:29)
1 Timothy 5:17
Proverbs 9:12
2 Chronicles 24:19

How did God show the youths both His discipline and His mercy?
God brought the bear to attack Israel.

D **Did You Ever . . . ?** You might be saying, "I'd never make fun of God's servants." Austin and Katie said the same thing until they thought back to some of their recent actions in church. Look at the pictures and decide if you have ever acted in similar ways toward one of God's servants. Write something you can do that will show more respect to God's servants.

Ha! Ha! Ha! Ha!

Wow, what an earful! She sounds like a screech owl, doesn't she?

Ugh! Pastor Ray is so boring. Isn't it time to go yet?

29

E **The "Prophet's Chamber."** The woman from Shunem went to great lengths to benefit Elisha. Read 2 Kings 4:9-10 and draw the room and furnishings the woman provided for Elisha.

Why did the Shunammite woman want to build a prophet's chamber for Elisha? Check the best reason and explain your choice of why you think she wanted to help Elisha.

_____ She felt sorry for Elisha and wanted to help him.

_____ She wanted to make sure he got his proper rest.

_____ She was honoring Elisha because he was God's servant.

_____

_____

Compare 2 Kings 4:9 and 1 Peter 4:9. Based on these Scriptures, the Shunammite woman's hospitality pleased God because of something she didn't do. Write it on the sign to the side.

F **Not Once . . . But Twice!** God rewarded the Shunammite woman not once but twice. Read the verses and complete the statements.

THE REWARD CARD

God rewarded her by

_____

(2 Kings 4:17)

God rewarded her by

_____

(2 Kings 4:32-37)

THE REWARD CARD

When I honor God's servants, I will be rewarded too because I will be working together with them

_____

_____

(3 John 8)

G **Shame on Naaman.** Dr. Diggit is exploring near the Jordan River to answer some questions about Naaman. Read 2 Kings 5:10-12 and circle the reasons why it was so hard for Naaman to follow Elisha's instructions.

1. Naaman thought Elisha charged too much for the cure.
2. Naaman wanted Elisha to come in person to him.
3. Naaman wanted to be healed instantly.
4. Naaman didn't like the way Elisha was dressed.
5. Naaman thought Elisha's rituals would bring the cure.
6. Naaman didn't have enough money to pay for the healing.
7. Naaman didn't think that seven dips were enough.
8. Naaman thought the rivers in his country were better.

H **The R_x for Naaman and You.** Finally, Naaman listened to God's servant, obeyed his orders and was healed. Read 2 Kings 5:13-16 and write your own journal entry of how Naaman might have felt before he was cured, what he did to be cured and how he felt afterward.

NAAMAN'S JOURNAL

Date: _____

_____
_____
_____
_____
_____

Do you ever have trouble, like Naaman did, in following the advice of God's servants? Color in the symbols ▲, ♦ and ♣ to see what Naaman needed to get rid of before he was healed and what we need to get rid of before we see God's power at work in our lives.

120

Isaiah: The Messianic Prophet

A
Isaiah's "Extra-Ordinary" Call. Isaiah's call to be God's servant was quite out of the ordinary. Read the verses in Isaiah 6 and follow the specific directions in each cloud.

What did Isaiah SEE?
God
Draw what Isaiah saw. (vs. 1-4)

What did Isaiah CONFESS?
his sins
List the things he confessed. (v. 5)

What did Isaiah NEED?
Isaiah needed for the Lord to forgive him
Complete the sentence. (vs. 6-7)

Who CALLED Isaiah to service?
God
Write the name on the line. (v. 8)

(speech bubbles on illustration:) "I also suck!" "I am stupid!" "I am also the loser in school!"

What did Isaiah SAY in response to the call?
go
Write his exact words. (v. 8)

B
Isaiah's "Extra-Ordinary" Message. All of Isaiah's prophecies came true just as he said, but three were the most amazing of all. Read the verses in Isaiah and fill in the missing names to the three prophecies.

Isaiah prophesied that . . .

1. Judah would be carried into captivity by _God_. (39:6)

2. _Judah_ would rebuild Jerusalem and the Temple. (44:28)

3. God would send one final Person He called _Isaiah_ who would bring lasting justice to the earth. (42:1)

If you were a modern day Isaiah, what would your message be to people?
_____

C **Perfectly Fulfilled.** Did you know the prophet Isaiah wrote more prophecies of Jesus Christ's first coming than any other writer in the Bible? Read the description of the prophecy concerning the Messiah. Write the reference that "predicts" the event and the one that "fulfills" it in the appropriate columns on the chart.

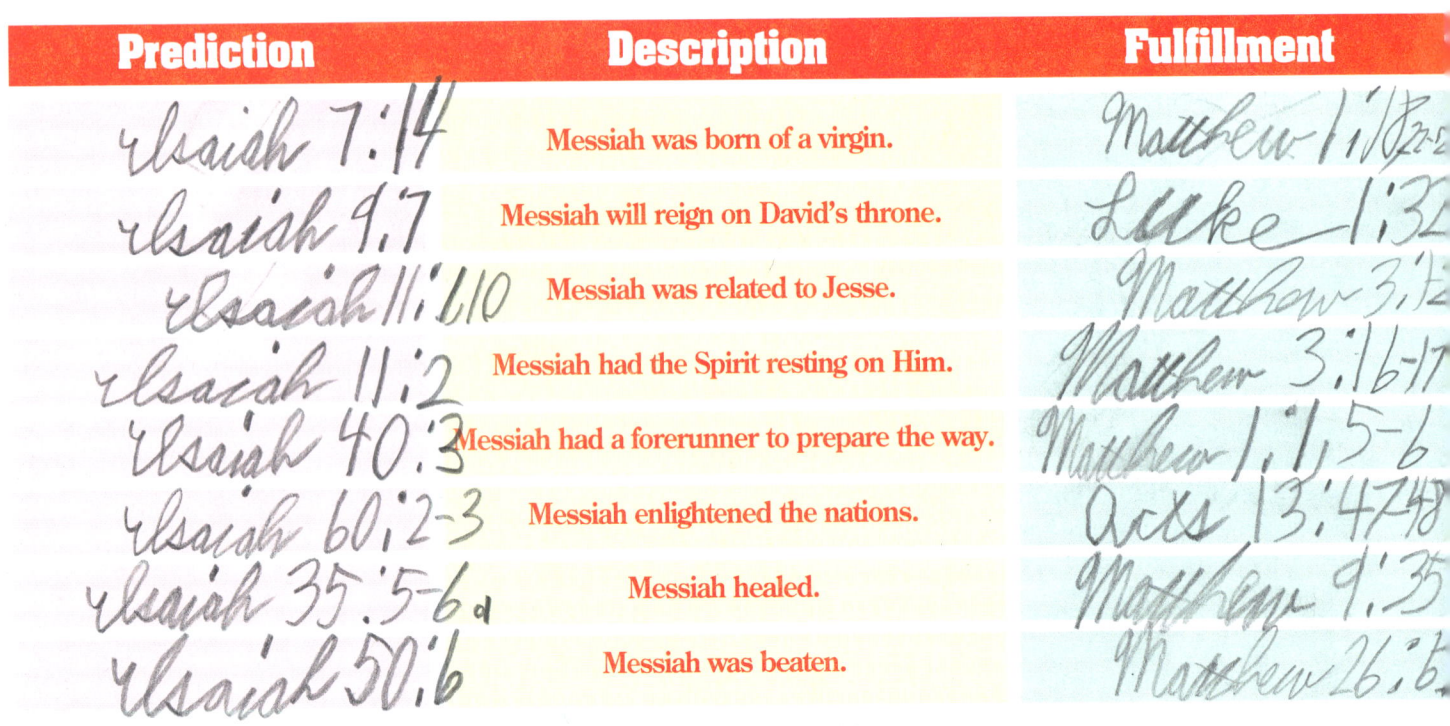

~~Isaiah 11:2~~ ~~Acts 13:47-48~~
~~Isaiah 11:1, 10~~ ~~Matthew 9:35~~
~~Isaiah 60:2-3~~ ~~Matthew 3:16-17~~
~~Isaiah 9:7~~ ~~Matthew 26:67~~
~~Isaiah 35:5-6a~~ ~~Matthew 1:1, 5-6~~
~~Isaiah 40:3~~ ~~Matthew 3:1-2~~
~~Isaiah 7:14~~ ~~Matthew 1:18, 22-23~~
~~Isaiah 50:6~~ ~~Luke 1:32~~

Prediction	Description	Fulfillment
Isaiah 7:14	Messiah was born of a virgin.	Matthew 1:18, 22-23
Isaiah 9:7	Messiah will reign on David's throne.	Luke 1:32
Isaiah 11:1, 10	Messiah was related to Jesse.	Matthew 1:1, 5-6
Isaiah 11:2	Messiah had the Spirit resting on Him.	Matthew 3:16-17
Isaiah 40:3	Messiah had a forerunner to prepare the way.	Matthew 3:1-2
Isaiah 60:2-3	Messiah enlightened the nations.	Acts 13:47-48
Isaiah 35:5-6a	Messiah healed.	Matthew 9:35
Isaiah 50:6	Messiah was beaten.	Matthew 26:67

D **Prophecies for the Future.** Isaiah also prophesied about the Second Coming of Christ. Read Isaiah 2:3-4; 25:1; 32:1; and 35:9-10. Write a description of what life will be like when Jesus comes again.

Life will be like excitement for those who made it to heaven. But for those who didn't it would be horrible.

E **One Lord . . . with Many Names.** God is so great that the Bible uses many names to describe His nature. But what was Isaiah's view of God? Using the verses in Isaiah, write the names the prophet used when he referred to God. Use your glossary to write the meaning in the space below the lines. Finally, practice saying the names the way we would if we translated them from the Hebrew language.

Lord (1:2a)
(Adonai)

God (1:10b)
(Elohim)

Everlasting God (40:28)
(Owlam Elohim)

Holy One (1:4b)
(Qadowshi)

Almighty (13:6b)
(El Shaddai)

Lord Almighty (1:9)
(Adonai Tsaba)

Rock Eternal (26:4)
(Owlam)

F **His Name Means . . . .** Choose one of the names of God and describe how the Lord has shown that particular attribute to you. Then think of another attribute of God and invent your own name for Him. Write it in the second box and tell why you chose it.

Holy One — God is the Holy One in the universe.

Holy Rock — God protects me all the time.

A Prophetic Puzzle. Approximately 300 years before Jesus was born, Isaiah made one of the most amazing prophecies about Christ's death and resurrection. Read through Isaiah 53 and the New Testament passages. Write the verse from Isaiah 53 that best fits each New Testament passage.

John 12:37 But although He had done so many signs before them, they did not believe in Him,

Isaiah 53:____

Philippians 2:5-7 ... Christ Jesus, who, being in the form of God, ... made Himself of no reputation, taking the form of a bondservant, *and* coming in the likeness of men.

Isaiah 53: ____

Matthew 27:57-60 Now when evening had come, there came a rich man ... asked for the body of Jesus... he wrapped it in a clean linen cloth, and laid it in his new tomb which he had hewn out of the rock;

Isaiah 53:____

Luke 23:24, 26, 33 So Pilate gave sentence ... they led Him away,... And when they had come to the place called Calvary, there they crucified Him,

Isaiah 53:____

Matthew 27:41, 43 Likewise the chief priests also, mocking with the scribes and elders, said, ... "He trusted in God; let Him deliver Him now if He will have Him;"

Isaiah 53:____

John 1:11 He came to His own, and His own did not receive Him.

Isaiah 53: ____

Matthew 27:12 And while He was being accused by the chief priests and elders, He answered nothing.

Isaiah 53:____

I Peter 3:18 For Christ also suffered once for sins, the just for the unjust, that He might bring us to God,....

Isaiah 53:____

Romans 3:23 For all have sinned and fall short of the glory of God,
2 Corinthians 5:21 For He (God) made Him (Christ)... *to be* sin for us,

Isaiah 53:_____

Jeremiah: God's Weeping Prophet

31

A **Keep in Mind God's Plan.** Do you know that God had a wonderful plan in mind for His people, Israel? God included Jeremiah in His plan before he was even born. Read Jeremiah 1 and fill in the blanks to see what God had planned for the prophet and how He prepared him for service.

For I know the thoughts that I think toward you, says the Lord, thoughts of peace and not of evil, to give you a future and a hope.
Jeremiah 29:11

I will arrange for a son named _____ to be born to _____, one of the _____ at Anathoth. Anathoth is close to Jerusalem where the priests and kings reside. (v. 1)

I will have Jeremiah minister especially to Judah's _____, its _____, its _____ and its _____. (v. 18)

I will call Jeremiah in the _____ year of King _____ reign. (v. 2) He will serve throughout the reigns of _____ and _____ until Judah is carried away into exile. (v. 3)

I will have Jeremiah _____ to _____ I send him and _____ whatever I command him to speak. (v. 7)

I will ordain Jeremiah to be a _____ to the _____ before he is _____ (v. 5) because of the people's _____. (v. 16)

I will tell him not to be _____ of them because I will be _____ him. (v. 8)

125

B DETOUR . . . Roadblock Ahead! Austin and Katie are having trouble understanding how God's wonderful plan for Jeremiah could include so many roadblocks. Read the verses in Jeremiah. In the "detour signs" circle the group or person who caused the roadblocks. On the arrows write what God did to deliver Jeremiah from the roadblocks.

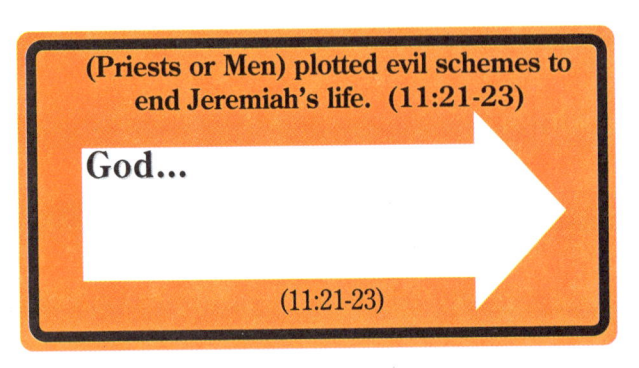

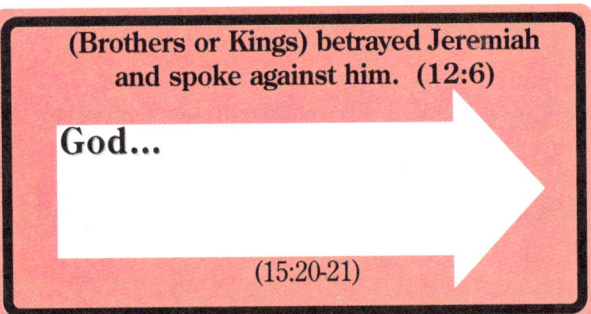

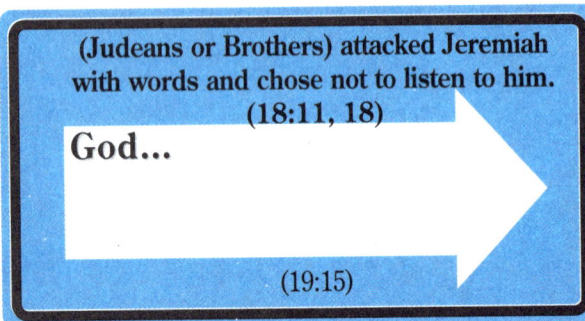

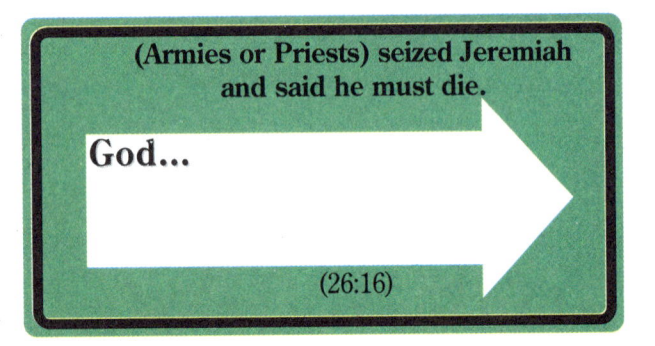

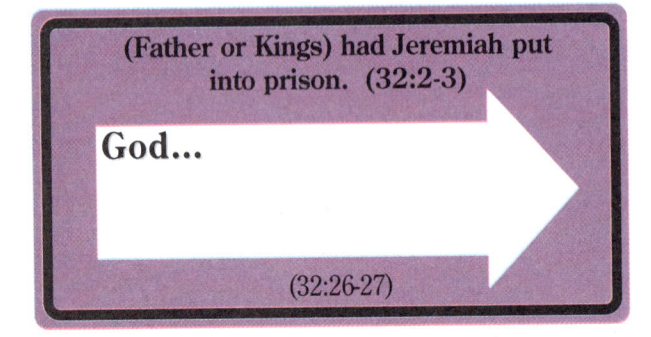

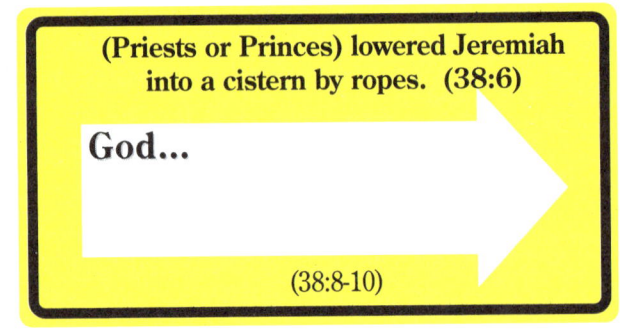

(Priests or Men) plotted evil schemes to end Jeremiah's life. (11:21-23)

God...

(11:21-23)

(Brothers or Kings) betrayed Jeremiah and spoke against him. (12:6)

God...

(15:20-21)

(Judeans or Brothers) attacked Jeremiah with words and chose not to listen to him. (18:11, 18)

God...

(19:15)

(Armies or Priests) seized Jeremiah and said he must die.

God...

(26:16)

(Father or Kings) had Jeremiah put into prison. (32:2-3)

God...

(32:26-27)

(Priests or Princes) lowered Jeremiah into a cistern by ropes. (38:6)

God...

(38:8-10)

C The Big Test. Why does God test your faith by allowing roadblocks? Read the verses in James and answer Katie and Austin's questions.

Why does God want to test my faith?

(1:3)

What happens if I pass the test?

(1:12)

DETOUR ROADBLOCK AHEAD

126

31

D **Keeping the "House Rules."** God sent Jeremiah to the house of the Rechabites to show Judah what being faithful to God meant. What are the choices you can make today that show your faithfulness to God?

1. Read Jeremiah 35:6-7 and list the ways the Rechabites were faithful in keeping the "house rules" of their earthly father, Jonadad.

_____
_____
_____
_____
_____

2. Think about some of the "house rules" your parents have established in your home. Then list some of the choices you can make to honor them.

_____
_____
_____
_____
_____

3. Read the following verses and write some of the ways you can be faithful to God, your Heavenly Father, by honoring some of His "house rules."

Hebrews 10:25 _____

2 Corinthians 9:7 _____

John 13:34 _____

1 Corinthians 4:2 _____

Colossians 3:20 _____

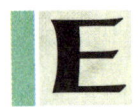

A Modern Day Jeremiah. Amy Carmichael had some things in common with the prophet Jeremiah. Read about Amy Carmichael's call in the letter she wrote to her mother. Shade in the phrases that show her trust in God's faithfulness. Underline the phrases that show her heart's desire, and put a wavy line under the phrases that illustrate her thoughts about the opposition she might have. Finally, read Jeremiah 1:4-5, 7; 2:11-13; 16:1-2; 20:7; and 32:26-27. Complete the paragraph comparing the lives of Jeremiah and Amy Carmichael. (You can also use the notes you took in class.)

January 14, 1892

My Precious Mother,

Have you given your child unreservedly to the Lord for whatever He wills? . . . . For a long time as you know the thought of those dying in the dark —— 50,000 of them every day, . . . has been very present with me, and the longing to go to them, and tell them of Jesus, has been strong upon me . . . . "Go Ye." I never heard it just so plainly before; . . . I know He spoke. He says "Go," I cannot stay . . . . Many difficulties have risen in my mind, they seem very great, the "crooked places" seem very crooked, but it seems to me that all He asks is that we should take the one step He shows us, and in simplest, most practical trust leave all results to Him . . . . I know that very few of our friends will think I am right. Those who don't know the Shepherd's Voice themselves will be quite sure I am very wrong and mistaken, but He has said, "Walk before Me, and be thou perfect." He knows, and He won't let me dishonour Him by making a mistake. . . . If it is His Will, I must do it . . . .

Your own Amy

(from: *Amy Carmichael of Dohnavur*, 1959)

Jeremiah and Amy Carmichael were alike because

Daniel: Excellent in Spirit

32

A **Divine Diet Food.** Daniel and his three friends made a decision about the food they would not eat when they were taken captive to Babylon. Read the "Food Facts" of both the Babylonians and Israelites. Then read Daniel 1:8-10. Fill in the conversations Daniel and his three friends might have had and the request he made to the king's official. Finally, answer the questions that follow.

Babylonian Food Facts

#1 The king's meat was usually given for sacrifices to pagan gods before it was served in the palace.

#2 Wine was served full strength with no water added to it.

Israelite Food Facts

#1 God had told Israel not to eat certain meats, especially the meat sacrificed to other gods.

#2 Water was usually added to wine to weaken its strength.

How did God bless Daniel and his three friends for standing alone? (Daniel 1:17-20)

_____

Can you think of a situation when you might need to stand alone for God? Decide what choices you will need to make beforehand and write about them below.

_____
_____

129

B Decoding the Dream. Dr. Diggit is trying to follow Daniel's interpretation of King Nebuchadnezzar's dream. Read Daniel 2:31-35 and write the materials used for the statue body parts. Use the information on the crowns to fill in the world kingdoms and principal rulers. Answer the questions below. (Clue: Since the chart is written in chronological order from top to bottom, start with the crown that lists the oldest kingdom.)

The Meaning of the Statue and the Stone

Statue Part	Material	World Kingdom	Ruler	Scripture (Daniel 2)
Head				(vs. 37-38)
Chest and Arms				(v. 39)
Stomach and Thighs				(v. 39)
Legs				(v. 40)
Feet			Antichrist	(vs. 41-43)
Stone	Cut without hands			(vs. 44-45)

CHRIST'S KINGDOM Jesus Christ — Future

ROME Tiberius and Gaius Gracchus 146 B.C. to A.D. 476

BABYLON Nebuchadnezzar 605 B.C. to 539 B.C.

GREECE Alexander the Great 331 B.C. to 146 B.C.

MEDO-PERSIA Darius 539 B.C. to 331 B.C.

What crushed the statue? _____ (vs. 34-35)

Which kingdom will never be destroyed? _____ (v. 44)

Which Ruler will live forever? _____ (v. 44)

32

C **Scrawl on the Wall.** The wisest men in Babylon were not able to read the "handwriting on the wall" to King Belshazzar. Use the code to write the English letter or letters to the left of each Hebrew letter. Then try to read the words from right to left. Read Daniel 5:25 to see if you have written them correctly. Using the verses in Daniel 5, write the word and its interpretation on the lines.

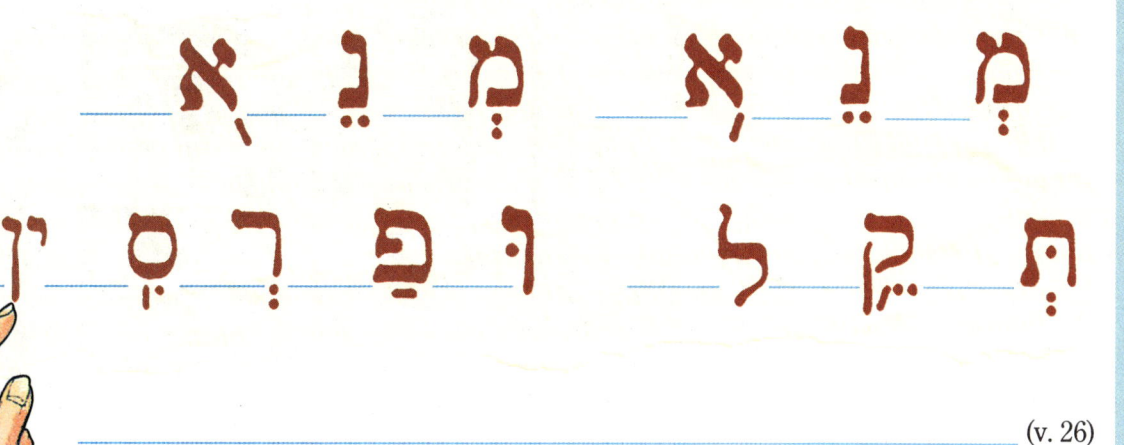

Code
מְ = Me
פַ = pha
תְ = Te
א = e
נֵ = n
ס = s
ר = r
קֵ = ke
ל = l
וּ = u
ין = in

מְ נֵ א   מְ נֵ א

תְ קֵ ל   וּ פַ ר ס ין

_____ (v. 26)
_____ (v. 27)
_____ (v. 28)

Who sent the fingers on the wall? (v. 25) _____

D **"Found Wanting" or Full?** Daniel and Belshazzar were very different. Read their descriptions of each other in Daniel 5:13-17, 22-28. Write a paragraph contrasting their differences.

_____
_____
_____
_____
_____
_____
_____

E **Packed with PACT?** Are your prayers packed with **PACT**? Do you remember what **PACT** stands for? Refresh your memory by working the crossword puzzle.

DOWN:

1. Something you are doing when you acknowledge the greatness of God.

3. Something you are doing when you tell God you've done wrong.

ACROSS:

2. Something you are doing when you are grateful to God.

4. Something you are doing when you have a need.

F **Check Out PACT.** One reason we know Daniel had an "excellent spirit" is because he included **PACT** in his prayer life. Read the verses from some of his prayers in Daniel. Then check in the box every time a passage includes "**P**" "**A**" "**C**" or "**T**." If Daniel mentions an attribute of God in the same passage, write it under "God's Attributes."

Reference	P	A	C	T	God's Attributes
2:20-23	☐	☐	☐	☐	
9:3-5	☐	☐	☐	☐	
9:5-8	☐	☐	☐	☐	
9:9-11	☐	☐	☐	☐	
9:12-14	☐	☐	☐	☐	
9:15-17	☐	☐	☐	☐	
9:18-19	☐	☐	☐	☐	

Now, think of a way you can pray a **PACT** prayer today. List some things you will include in your prayer.

P _____   **A** _____

C _____   **T** _____

Ezra: The Religious Reformer

33

A **Outlining Ezra's Biography.** Austin and Katie are trying to find some information in the Bible to write a brief biography about Ezra. Read the verses and answer the questions, then on another sheet of paper use the information from your outline to write a three paragraph biography about Ezra's life.

Outline for Ezra

I. **Ezra's Background**

  A. Who was his father? _____ (7:1)

  B. Where did he grow up and live? _____ (7:6)

  C. From what priestly line was he? _____ (7:13)

  D. Which famous priest was his descendant?
   _____ (7:5)

II. **Ezra's Ministry**

  A. Who granted permission for his return? _____ (7:12-13)

  B. Why did he return to Jerusalem? _____
   _____ (7:27)

  C. When did he return to Jerusalem? _____
   _____ (7:9)

  D. What were his jobs? _____ (7:11)

III. **Ezra's Character**

  A. What was his heart's desire? _____
   _____ (7:10)

  B. What did he possess? _____ (7:25)

  C. What did he do for guidance? _____ (8:23)

  D. What did he confess? _____ (9:5-6)

  E. How did his humble example affect others? _____ (10:1-2)

  F. What was true about his leadership? _____ (10:10-12)

B **The People Respond.** Dr. Diggit has discovered how God's people responded to God's Word. Read the verses in Nehemiah. Complete his answers by writing a word that fits in the boxes. The word in the shaded area will tell you what the people did when they heard Ezra read the Law.

When the people heard the Law, they
_____ . (8:9)

The people listened to the Word from
morning till _____ . (8:3)

The people asked _____ to read
God's Word. (8:1)

The people rejoiced when they heard God's
Word because they _____
it. (8:11-12)

The people lifted their _____
and worshiped when they heard God's Word.
(8:6)

As the Word was being read, the people gave
it their full _____ . (8:3)

When the people stood up to hear God's Word, they were showing _____ to God. (8:5)

C **How Do I Respond?** Think about the people's response to God's Word. Then list some of the choices God wants you to make when you hear or read God's Word. The first one has been done for you.

When I hear or read the Word of God...

   1. I should give it my full attention.

   2. _____

   3. _____

D **Worship That Pleases God.** Ezra taught God's people the Scriptures and then led them in worshiping God in a way that pleased Him. Use your glossary to complete the definition of the word **worship**. Study the two examples from the Bible. Put a wavy line under the phrases that praise God for His attributes and circle the phrases that praise God for the things He has done.

Worship means to _____

Old Testament

Blessed be Your glorious name, which is exalted above all blessing and praise! You alone are the Lord; You have made Heaven, the Heaven of heavens, with all their host, the earth and everything on it, the seas and all that is in them, and You preserve them all. The host of Heaven worships You.

Nehemiah 9:5b-6

New Testament

You are worthy, O Lord, to receive glory and honor and power; for You created all things, and by Your will they exist and were created. Worthy is the Lamb who was slain to receive power and riches and wisdom, and strength and honor and glory and blessing!

Revelation 4:11; 5:12

E **In Other Words — Worship.** Using the verses, find attributes of God to complete the acrostic for worship.

_____ **W** (Romans 16:27)
_____ **O** (Deuteronomy 6:4)
_____ **R** (Ezra 9:15)
_____ **S** (1 Timothy 2:3)
_____ **H** (Revelation 4:8)
_____ **I** (1 Timothy 1:17)
_____ **P** (Matthew 5:48)

F **The Silence That Was Heard.** What was happening during the "400 Silent Years" between the Old and New Testaments? Even though God wasn't speaking directly through His prophets, He was preparing the world for the coming of the Messiah. To find how God was working, match the letters of the historical events with the statements.

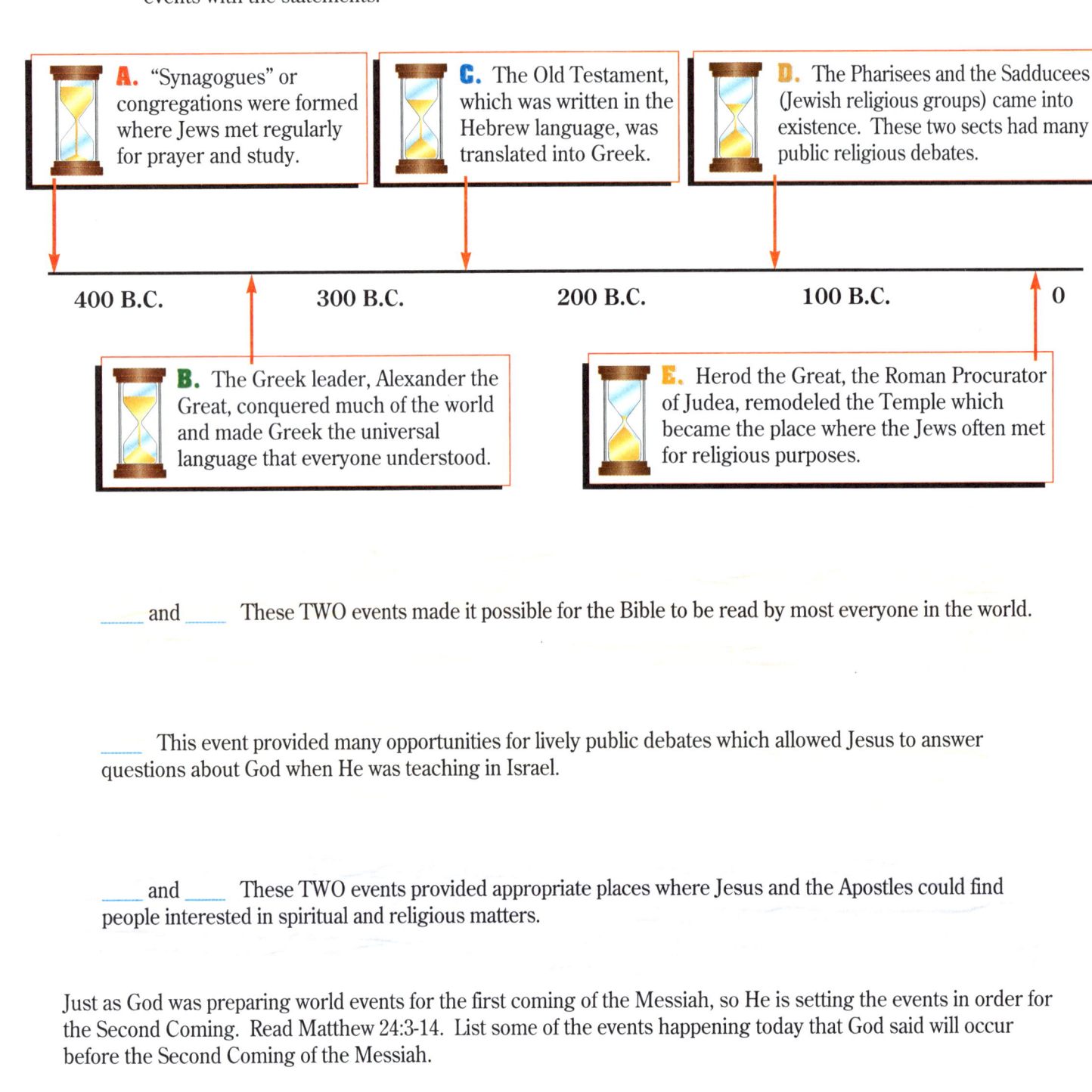

A. "Synagogues" or congregations were formed where Jews met regularly for prayer and study.

C. The Old Testament, which was written in the Hebrew language, was translated into Greek.

D. The Pharisees and the Sadducees (Jewish religious groups) came into existence. These two sects had many public religious debates.

400 B.C.　　　300 B.C.　　　200 B.C.　　　100 B.C.　　　0

B. The Greek leader, Alexander the Great, conquered much of the world and made Greek the universal language that everyone understood.

E. Herod the Great, the Roman Procurator of Judea, remodeled the Temple which became the place where the Jews often met for religious purposes.

____ and ____ These TWO events made it possible for the Bible to be read by most everyone in the world.

____ This event provided many opportunities for lively public debates which allowed Jesus to answer questions about God when He was teaching in Israel.

____ and ____ These TWO events provided appropriate places where Jesus and the Apostles could find people interested in spiritual and religious matters.

Just as God was preparing world events for the first coming of the Messiah, so He is setting the events in order for the Second Coming. Read Matthew 24:3-14. List some of the events happening today that God said will occur before the Second Coming of the Messiah.

_____

_____

_____

Nehemiah: The Rebuilder

34

A

Who Am I? God used several leaders at different times to rebuild the Temple and restore the walls of Jerusalem. Match the description to the verse and then to the person by connecting the dots to all three.

WHO AM I? I prophesied that Cyrus would help build Jerusalem and lay the foundations for the Temple.

WHO AM I? I led a great revival by reading the Book of the Law all morning in front of the people.

WHO AM I? I prophesied that after 70 years of captivity the Jews would return to Jerusalem.

WHO AM I? I brought comforting messages from the Lord to those who were rebuilding the Temple.

WHO AM I? I cried to the Lord and prayed when I heard the walls around Jerusalem were broken.

WHO AM I? I was used of God (along with others) to actually work on the rebuilding of the Temple.

WHO AM I? I issued a proclamation to have the Temple in Jerusalem rebuilt.

- Haggai 1:13
- Ezra 5:2
- Nehemiah 8:2-3
- Nehemiah 1:3-4
- Isaiah 44:28
- Ezra 1:1-2
- Jeremiah 29:10

- Haggai
- Cyrus 
- Zerubbabel 
- Isaiah 
- Nehemiah 
- Ezra 
- Jeremiah 

Think of one Christian leader God is using to accomplish His purposes in your life. Complete the following sentence.

God is using _____ to accomplish His purposes in my life by _____, _____ and _____.

137

B **Arrows of Opposition.** Each time Nehemiah had opposition, he used just the right weapon from God's arsenal. Read the verses in Nehemiah. Write the appropriate word from the "Opposition Word Bank" on each arrow and the appropriate word from the "Arsenal Word Bank" on the shield to see how Nehemiah resisted his opposition.

Opposition Word Bank
Internal Greed
Plotting
Conspiracies
Ridicule
Fear of Attack
Discouragement

Arsenal Word Bank
Faith
Prayer for Strength
Stop Sinning: Usury
Alertness
Prayer for Punishment
Prayer and Alertness

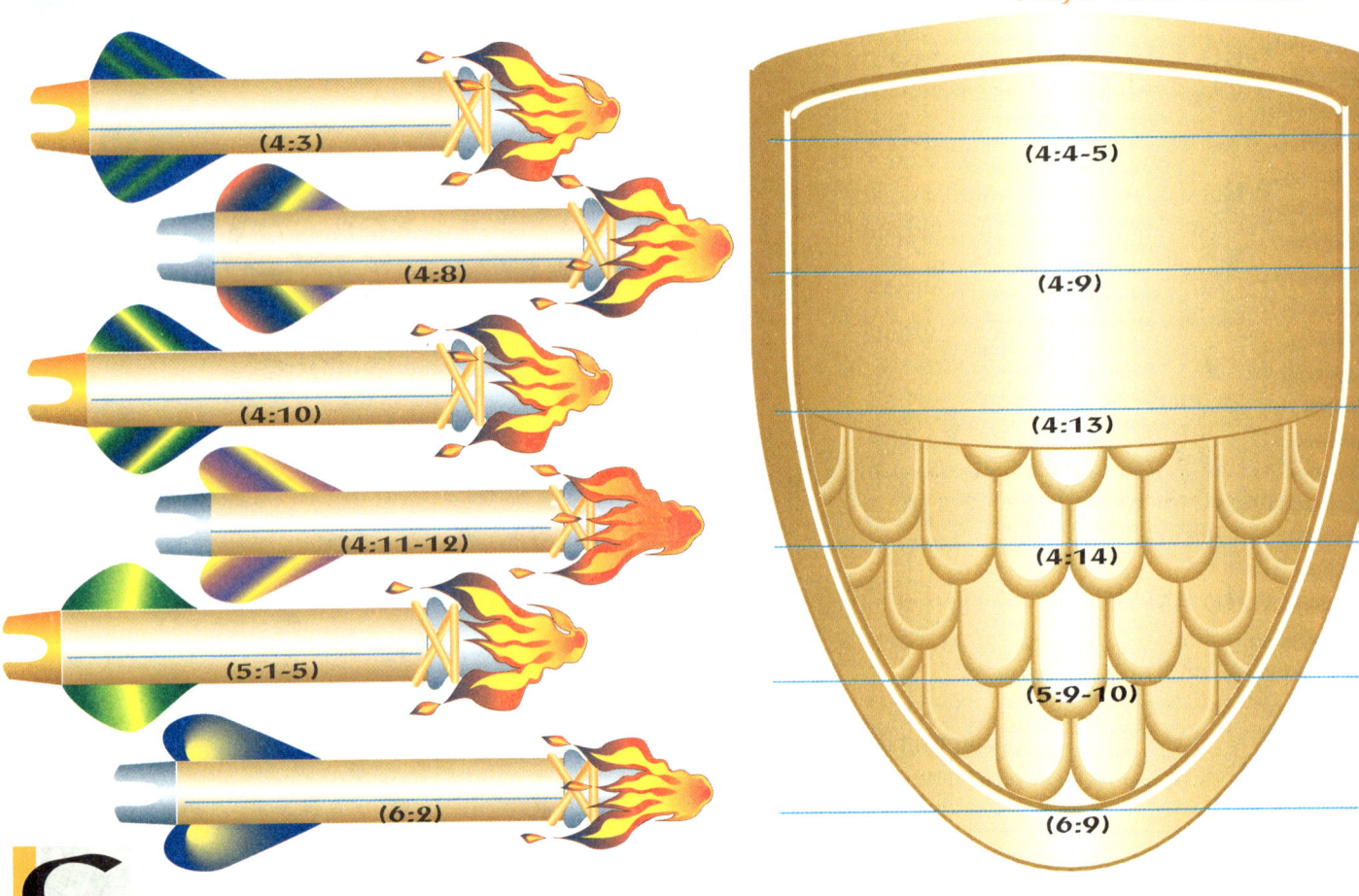

(4:3)
(4:8)
(4:10)
(4:11-12)
(5:1-5)
(6:2)

(4:4-5)
(4:9)
(4:13)
(4:14)
(5:9-10)
(6:9)

C **Using God's Arsenal.** Think of a time when God has helped you face opposition as you've tried to do His will. Compose a prayer to God thanking Him for the weapons He gave you to use.

What was Nehemiah's primary weapon in his arsenal against opposition to doing God's will?

What is yours?

34

D **Nothing but the Truth.** Who usually causes opposition when you are trying to do God's will? Help Austin and Katie find the truth about our worst enemy by reading the verses and circling the "**T**" for **true** or the "**F**" for **false**. If the statements are false, make them true by crossing out and/or adding words.

1. A name we sometimes call our enemy is Belshazzar. (2 Corinthians 2:11) — T F

2. Our enemy has blinded the eyes of unbelievers. (2 Corinthians 4:4) — T F

3. The devil is a murderer who tells lies. (John 8:44) — T F

4. To stand against the devil, we need to go to church. (Ephesians 6:11) — T F

5. Satan pretends to be an angel of darkness. (2 Corinthians 11:14) — T F

6. The Bible says Satan is like a roaring lion. (1 Peter 5:8) — T F

7. The devil is sometimes called prince of the universe. (John 14:30) — T F

8. Satan has absolutely no power to work miracles. (2 Thessalonians 2:9) — T F

9. The devil tries to stop the work of God's people. (1 Thessalonians 2:18) — T F

10. The devil will spend eternity in the Lake of Fire. (Revelation 20:10) — T F

Use the Morse Code to find the two things God wants us to do to fight the opposition that comes from our worst enemy.

.— . ... —   — .... .

—.. . ...— .—..   **and**

..—.. .— .—. —— .— .—. ....

——. —— —.. .— —.. ..—..

James 4:7-8

CODE
a .—	n —.
d —..	o ———
e .	r .—.
G ——.	s ...
h	t —
i ..	v ...—
l .—..	w .——

E **Leading in Leadership.** Sometimes you can tell what character qualities someone has by what he says to others. Using the verses from Nehemiah, fill in the leadership qualities that fit the blanks on the small banners. (Some of the letters have been written in for you.) Inside the big banner write the one word you think best describes Nehemiah as a leader.

Nehemiah, a _____ Leader

A man of
__ __ __ i __ __ __ __
(4:14)

A man who
e__ __ c__ __ __ __ __ __ __ed
others
(2:20; 8:10)

A man of
s __ __ __ __ __ __ __ th
(5:6-7)

A man of
__ __ __ __ y __
(1:4-5)

F **Narrowing Our Priorities.** Which Christian leadership quality does God want you to mature in this week? Follow the directions in the different boxes to determine areas of leadership that you need to strengthen.

Add two leadership qualities to the list below.
A. faithfulness
B. honesty
C. endurance
D. courage
E. _____
F. _____

Circle the quality you are stronger in.

A or B	B or F
A or C	C or D
A or D	C or E
A or E	C or F
A or F	D or E
B or C	D or F
B or D	E or F
B or E	

Count all your A's, B's, C's, D's, E's and F's and write the number to the side of each letter.
A _____
B _____
C _____
D _____
E _____
F _____

Arrange your letters in priority order by putting the letter with the lowest number at the top and the highest at the bottom. The quality at the top will be the one you most need to work on.
_____
_____
_____
_____
_____
_____

140

Jesus Christ in the Old Testament

35

A **Our Messiah-King.** Jesus Christ fulfilled the Old Testament prophecies concerning the coming of the Messiah-King. Read the verses. Then match each prediction to the Old Testament prophecy and to the New Testament fulfillment.

Old Testament Prophecy	The Prediction	New Testament Fulfillment
Psalm 118:22	Messiah will be born in Bethlehem.	Luke 23:34
Zechariah 11:12	Messiah will be betrayed by a friend.	Luke 2:11
Psalm 22:18	Messiah will be rejected.	Matthew 26:15
Micah 5:2	Messiah will be placed with sinners.	Luke 20:17
Psalm 41:9	Messiah will be sold for 30 pieces of silver.	Luke 22:37
Isaiah 53:12	Messiah's garments will be gambled away.	Matthew 10:4

B **A Logical Conclusion.** Austin's friend, Bruce, is having trouble really believing in the truth of Matthew 25:31 and Acts 1:11. Read the verses to complete Bruce's statement. Using what you learned in Exercise A, write something logical that Austin might say to convince Bruce that the prophecy he is concerned about will also come true.

I don't know, Austin. It's hard to believe that Jesus, God's Son, will really _____.

I know, Bruce. But just think, Jesus Christ _____

C **Which Priest Did It?** Contrast the priesthood in the Old Testament with the priesthood of Jesus Christ. Fill in the words from Hebrews 9 that complete the statements about the two priesthoods.

THE OLD TESTAMENT HIGH PRIEST . . .

ministered in an _____ sanctuary. (v. 1)

made an offering for _____ and _____. (v. 7)

offered the blood of _____ and bulls. (v. 13)

entered the Most Holy Place _____ a year. (v. 7)

THE NEW TESTAMENT HIGH PRIEST (JESUS CHRIST) . . .

entered into a sanctuary in _____. (v. 24)

made an offering for the sins of _____. (v. 28)

offered _____ blood. (v. 12)

entered into the Most Holy Place _____ for all. (v. 12)

D **Our High Priest, Jesus.** One of the priestly ministries of Jesus is His intercessory prayer for us. What do you think He's praying for you? Read John 17:11, 15, 24 and 1 John 2:1-2. Put a check by the things for which Jesus, your High Priest, is praying for you. Then complete the statement.

_____ Jesus asks God to forgive me for my sins.

_____ Jesus asks God to bless me with material goods.

_____ Jesus asks God to protect me against my enemy, Satan.

_____ Jesus asks God to give me good friends.

_____ Jesus asks God to keep me with Him where He is.

It is comforting to know that Jesus is my High Priest because _____

_____

_____

_____

35

E **Our Superior Teacher, Christ.** Jesus explained the teachings of the Old Testament by clearly revealing their full meanings. Read the verses in Matthew 5 and write the phrase or sentence that contrasts the "letter of the Law" with the "spirit of the Law." Unscramble the words to see what Jesus included when He taught "the spirit of the Law."

LETTER OF THE LAW

(v. 21) _____
(v. 27) _____
(v. 38) _____
(v. 43) _____

SPIRIT OF THE LAW

(v. 22) _____
(v. 28) _____
(v. 39) _____
(v. 44) _____

Jesus made the teaching of the Law clear by including not just what we do and say but also _____ _____ _____ .
                                                  rou   rnien   sotugthh

F **Report Card Time.** Suppose you were a teacher who graded your students on the way they obeyed the teachings of Christ. Read Millie's "test results." Write the grade you think she deserves in the two subjects. On the comment lines, write your reason for grading her the way you did.

SCHOOL OF LIFE	REPORT CARD	NAME: MILLIE
Subject	Actions and Thoughts: Test Results	Grades
"Letter of the Law"	"At school, I have done kind deeds and said nice things to Shannon."	
"Spirit of the Law"	"No one has to know I really don't like Shannon at all."	

Comments: _____
_____
_____

143

G **Seeing Jesus as God.** Some people don't believe that Jesus and Jehovah God of the Old Testament are the same God. But one way to see They are the same is to compare some of Their characteristics. Read the verses and write the letter of the reference in the correct column to see if they have the same characteristics.

Characteristic	God or Lord	Jesus	Verse Bank
He is the great "I AM."			a. Isaiah 40:28
He is the good Shepherd.			b. John 10:7, 11
He forgives sins.			c. John 8:58
He is the Creator God.			d. Jeremiah 31:34
			e. Psalm 23:1
			f. Colossians 1:15-16
			g. Exodus 3:14
			h. Mark 2:5, 10

H **Graph Jesus' Message.** Jesus gave a very important message in the book of John. Write His message on the lines below by finding the letters at each point. Use the first number in the pair to find the letter on the "X" and the second number to find the letter on the "Y." Then read the reference to see if you wrote the message correctly.

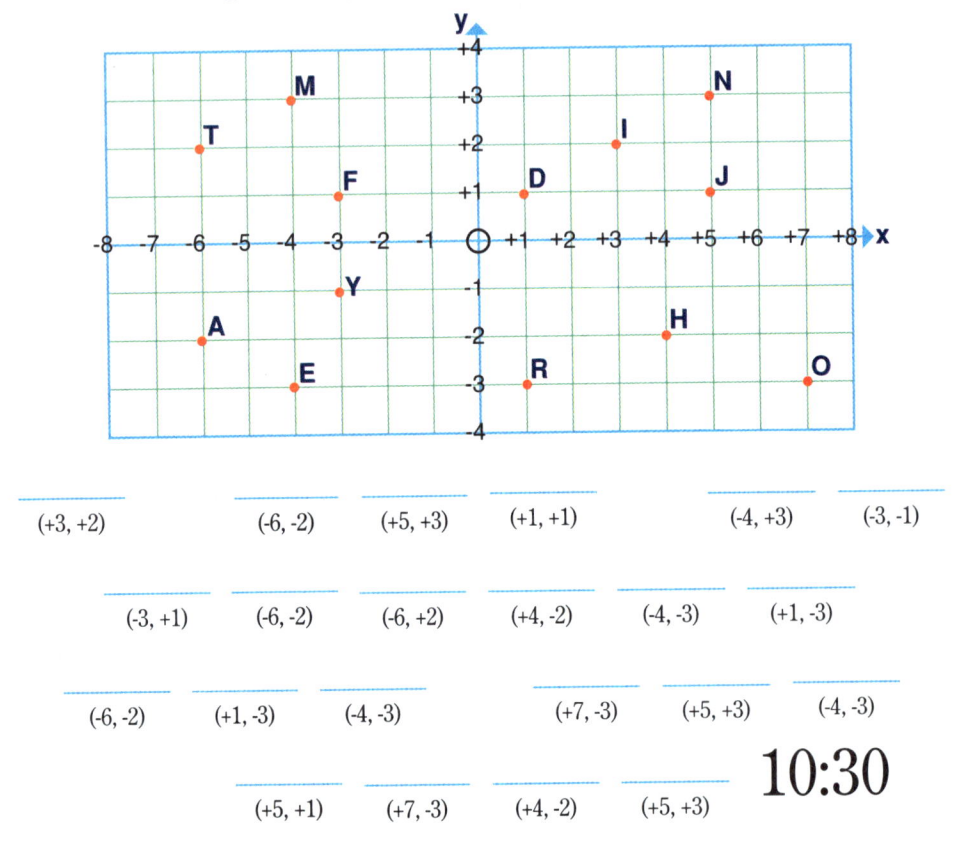

___ ___ ___ ___ ___ ___
(+3, +2) (-6, -2) (+5, +3) (+1, +1) (-4, +3) (-3, -1)

___ ___ ___ ___ ___ ___
(-3, +1) (-6, -2) (-6, +2) (+4, -2) (-4, -3) (+1, -3)

___ ___ ___ ___ ___ ___
(-6, -2) (+1, -3) (-4, -3) (+7, -3) (+5, +3) (-4, -3)

___ ___ ___ ___
(+5, +1) (+7, -3) (+4, -2) (+5, +3)

10:30

144

Overview of the Old Testament

36

A

Let's Try to Remember. Do you remember how you began the year by learning that God made the first choices? He chose to reveal His Person, plan of redemption and principles for living in His special revelation, the Bible. Follow the instructions to answer the questions.

1. What have you learned about **GOD'S PERSON?** Draw a line through the five attributes you know are true of God.

H	M	E	F	T	I	A	F
O	O	R	C	H	S	O	V
L	O	V	I	N	G	H	G	I	R	L	I	F	E	R	E
L	S	U	O	E	T	L	O	V	I	M	Y	U	L	E	R

2. What did you learn about **GOD'S PLAN** of redemption? Fill in one of the most important truths you have learned this year in our Old Testament study.

Without the shedding of _____ there is no _____ of sin.
(Hebrews 9:22; Leviticus 17:11)

3. What did you learn about **GOD'S PRINCIPLES** for living? Match each subject with the best predicate to review some of the principles you learned.

Although God is invisible, I	is possible through God's Spirit.
To fight my enemy Satan, I	know He exists through revelation.
All of God's many promises	will help me in times of trial.
Trusting in God's sovereignty	is the beginning of wisdom.
Meditating on God's Word	is right because Christ forgave me.
Living the Christian life	should use God's armor and pray.
Reverent fear of the Lord	includes thinking it and doing it.
Choosing to forget others' debts	are true because He is faithful.

The Big Picture. Fill in as your teacher directs.

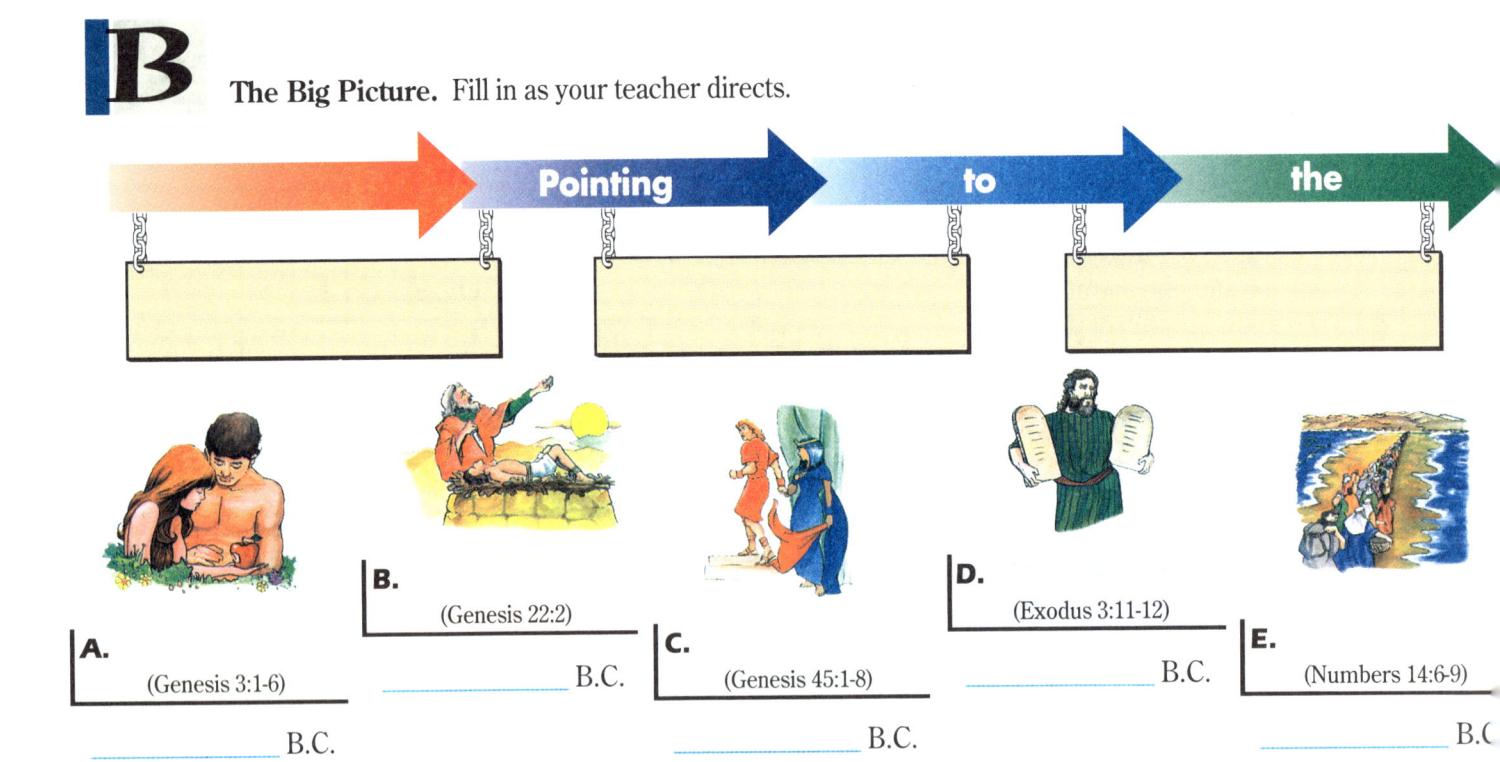

Pointing → to → the →

A. _____ (Genesis 3:1-6)
_____ B.C.

B. _____ (Genesis 22:2)
_____ B.C.

C. _____ (Genesis 45:1-8)
_____ B.C.

D. _____ (Exodus 3:11-12)
_____ B.C.

E. _____ (Numbers 14:6-9)
_____ B.C.

CHOICES

____ Chose to trust God even when he was asked to sacrifice his son

____ Chose to run from evil, and then later forgave his brothers who almost had him killed

____ Chose to disobey God's instructions in the Garden

____ Chose to help the nation Israel escape from Egyptian bondage

____ Chose to trust God rather than be afraid of the hard trials in the Promised Land

CONSEQUENCES

Became the leader who led Israel into the Promised land

Sin entered the world

Became known as the "Friend of God"

Became an example of God's forgiveness and saved his brothers from famine

Became Israel's deliverer out of Egypt

Review the promises God made to Abraham in Genesis 12:1-3. How were "all the families of the earth" blessed through Abraham?

_____
_____
_____

Check Galatians 3:14 to see if your answer is correct.

36

C The Big Picture Continued. Fill in as your teacher directs.

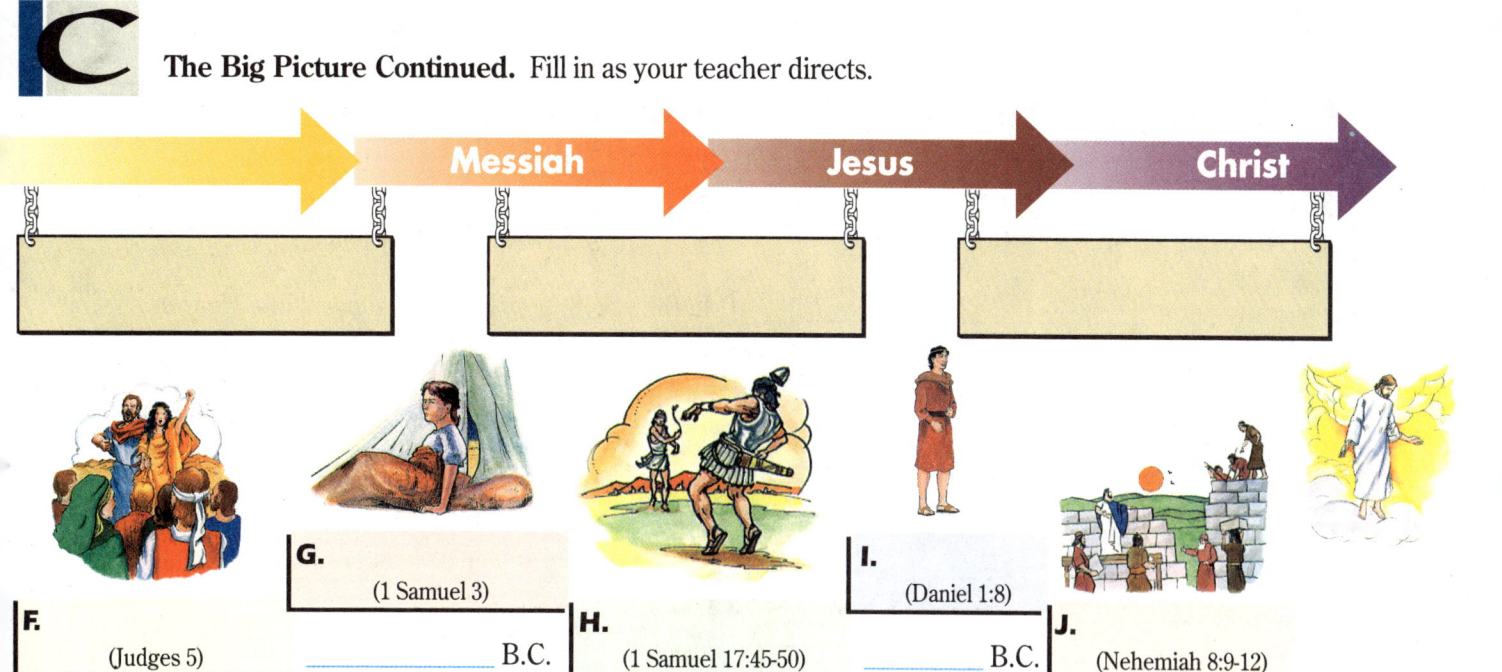

Messiah → Jesus → Christ

F. _____ (Judges 5) _____ B.C.

G. _____ (1 Samuel 3) _____ B.C.

H. _____ (1 Samuel 17:45-50) _____ B.C.

I. _____ (Daniel 1:8) _____ B.C.

J. _____ (Nehemiah 8:9-12) _____ B.C.

CHOICES

____ Chose to be faithful to his convictions rather than please the king of Babylon

____ Chose to listen and to obey the call of God

____ Chose to lead God's people when the men were too fearful

____ Chose to trust God and face the giant Philistine

____ Chose to rebuild God's reputation by restoring the walls of Jerusalem

CONSEQUENCES

Became the governor of Israel and helped to lead in a revival

Became the king who had a heart for God

Became a judge, priest and prophet over Israel and anointed the first king

Became the only woman judge and revealed her faith in a beautiful song of praise

Was given amazing prophecies about the future of the nations

How do the prophecies of the first coming of Christ help us to know that God will keep His promises to send His Son again a second time?

_____
_____

Read 2 Peter 3:13-14 to see what our response should be to God's promise of sending His Son.

_____
_____

147

D **What About You?** The most important choice you will ever make is to receive God's Son, Jesus Christ, as your own personal Savior. Read the verses and complete the truths about God's plan of redemption for you.

Because God is _____ (Psalm 99:9) and righteous,

only _____ (Matthew 5:48) people will be allowed into Heaven.

Sinners will be punished by spiritual _____ (Romans 6:23).

But because God has _____ (1 John 4:16),

mercy and _____ (1 Corinthians 1:3),

He desires to _____ (1 Corinthians 1:21)

the sinner from judgment

and prepare for him or her

a home in _____.

(Philippians 3:20)

God's plan of redemption

is to provide a substitute for your sins,

a blood _____

(Ephesians 5:2)

When you receive Jesus Christ by faith,

then you will have eternal life in Heaven.

God's Word says that we can become children of God by faith.

If you've never trusted in Christ, you can make the most important choice you'll ever make right now. Just confess your sins to God and believe that Jesus Christ, God's Son, died in your place as your substitute.

Then, after you receive Christ, remember that God enables you to make wise choices, through the power of His Holy Spirit, by reading and obeying the Bible and praying to God often. The choice is yours! God bless you!

Reference Section

Glossary

Concordance

Maps

♦ Glossary ♦

Aa

Abel - second son of Adam and Eve.

abomination - something that is hated.

Abraham - originally called Abram; father of the Hebrew tribe.

adversary - enemy.

Almighty - Translated "El Shaddai" (shad-dah'-ee), meaning the most powerful God.

ambitious - having a great desire to succeed in something.

Cc

Cain - first son of Adam and Eve who murdered his brother Abel.

conspiracy - a secret plan to commit a crime or wrong doing.

correction - adjusting to a standard.

covenant - an agreement between two persons or groups.

conviction - a very strong belief.

crafty - deceptively skillful.

cubit - a measurement of length measuring 18 inches or 0.5 meters.

cunning - crafty.

Dd

David - a godly king who moved Israel's place of worship to Bethlehem in preparation for the Messiah. David wrote most of the Psalms.

deception - using trickery.

discernment - the ability to distinguish right from wrong.

doctrine - principles or teachings.

Ee

emotion - a person's feelings, like love, hate or sadness.

enmity - hatred.

envy - desiring another's possessions or advantages.

eternal - no beginning or end; lasting forever.

Everlasting Strength - Translated "Owlam" (o-lawn'), meaning lasting forever.

Gg

Garden of Eden - first home of Adam and Eve.

God - Translated "Elohim" (el-o-heem'), meaning the God of truth.

grace - undeserved favor.

Hh

hallowed - highly respected and reverenced; set apart.

hin - a liquid measurement of approximately six pints.

Holy One - Translated "Qadowshi" (kaw-doshe'), meaning sacred and set apart.

humility - the characteristic of being meek, modest or submissive.

hyssop - - a small bush usually used in connection with blood and water in ceremonies to symbolize purification from sin and diseases.

Ii

immortal - not able to die; living forever.

inspiration - the way God divinely guided man to write the Bible.

instruction - a lesson.

intellect - a person's ability to reason or know.

Jj

jealousy - a spirit of fearfulness of being replaced by another or losing something.

Jew - a descendent of Abraham, Isaac and Jacob.

Kk

kinsman-redeemer - one who redeems the widow of a near relative by buying property and marrying her.

knowledge - acquiring facts and ideas through study, observation, and experience.

Ll

Lord - Translated "Adonai" (ad-o-noy'), meaning the existing God.

Lord of Hosts - Translated "Adonai Tsaba" (tsaw-baw), meaning Lord of all the heavenly hosts.

Lot - Abraham's nephew.

loyalty - the state of being devoted and faithful to a person or cause.

Mm

materialism - an excessive interest in worldly goods and concerns.

meditation - the exercise of the mind reflecting on religious matters.

mercy - an attribute of God that shows love to people even though they are unworthy.

missionary - one who is sent to tell others about God.

Nn

Nazarite - one who has taken a special vow not to cut hair, not to drink fermented beverages and not to touch dead bodies in order to be set apart unto God's service.

Noah - man who built an ark and survived the Flood.

Pp

pagan - one who is not a Christian.

parable - a story illustrating a religious truth.

pride - a high opinion of one's self. Conceited and puffed up.

providence - God's continual care over His creation in order to preserve and govern it.

purity - the quality for being free from sin.

Rr

rebellion - an act of opposition or an uprising against those in authority.

rebuke - to reprimand sharply.

redemption - salvation from sin purchased by the blood of Christ.

repentance - the act of changing one's mind about sin; to turn away from sin.

reproof - to rebuke for a misdeed.

revelation - information that is revealed which is not formerly known. God made Himself known to man through the Bible, His special revelation.

Ss

sacrifice - the offering of something to God for propitiation or forgiveness of sins.

Satan - a name for the devil meaning adversary.

Saul - the king who established kingdom rule over Israel and reigned for 15 years.

serpent - another name for the devil.

shekel - a measurement of weight approximately ten penny weights.

Sodom - a wicked city destroyed by God with fire.

Solomon - the son of David who reigned as king for 40 years and wrote the Proverbs, Ecclesiastes and the Song of Solomon.

sovereignty - an attribute of God that refers to His supreme authority and rule over all matters.

span - a measurement of length measuring 9 inches or 23 centimeters.

Tt

Theophany - an appearance of Christ prior to His earthly birth.

Uu

understanding - the ability to mentally grasp concepts.

unity - the state of being one and single-minded for a particular purpose.

Ur - Abraham's native city.

Vv

values - principles regarded as desirable.

vow - a religious promise made about doing something specific or abstaining from a particular activity.

Ww

will - a person's ability to choose.

wisdom - the skill of using past experience and knowledge about God to make good judgements or right choices.

worship - attributing worth to God.

♦ Concordance ♦

Aa

advice (advise, adviser, counsel)

1 Kings 12:8	he rejected the *a*
Proverbs 12:5	the *c* of the wicked
Proverbs 11:14	in the multitude of *c*
Proverbs 12:15	he who heeds *c* is wise
2 Corinthians 8:10	in this I give my *a*

angel (angels)

Genesis 16:7	Now the *A* of the Lord
Exodus 23:20	Behold, I send an *A*
Luke 2:9	And behold, and *a*
Luke 20:36	are equal to the *a*
Galatians 1:8	even if we, or an *a*
1 Peter 1:12	things which *a* desire

anoint (anointed, anointing)

1 Samuel 15:1	The Lord sent me to *a* you king
Psalm 23:5	*a* my head with oil
Isaiah 61:1	because the Lord has *a*
Luke 4:18	Because he has *a*
1 John 2:20	But you have an *a*

armor

Jeremiah 46:4	spears, put on the *a*
Romans 13:12	let us put on the *a*
Ephesians 6:11	Put on the whole *a*

awesome

Genesis 28:17	*a* is this place
Exodus 34:10	*a* thing that I will do
Psalm 66:3	*a* are Your works
Psalm 68:35	O God, You are more *a*
Psalm 99:3	Your great and *a* name
Isaiah 64:3	When You did *a* things

Bb

baptize (baptized, baptism)

Matthew 3:13	be *b* by him
Mark 16:16	*b* will be saved
1 Corinthians 12:13	by one Spirit *b* into
Acts 18:8	believe and were *b*
Romans 6:3	were *b* into Christ
Ephesians 4:5	one faith, one *b*

believe (believed, believes)

John 11:27	I *b* your are the Christ
Acts 16:31	*B* on the Lord Jesus Christ
Hebrews 11:6	comes to God must *b*
2 Timothy 1:12	I know whom I have *b*
1 Corinthians 13:7	*b* all things

born (birth)

Matthew 1:18	Now the *b* of Jesus
Luke 1:14	will rejoice at His *b*
Ecclesiastes 3:2	a time to be *b*
Isaiah 9:6	unto us a child is *b*
John 3:3	unless one is *b* again
1 John 4:7	who loves is *b* of God

bless (blessing, blessed)

Psalm 1:1	*B* is the man who walks
Psalm 132:5	I will abundantly *b*
Matthew 5:3	*B* are the
Galatians 3:14	that the *b* of Abraham
Hebrews 12:17	to inherit the *b*

blood

Leviticus 17:11	*b* that makes
Matthew 26:28	For this is My *b*
John 6:54	*b* has eternal life
Romans 5:9	justified by His *b*
Ephesians 6:12	against flesh and *b*
Revelation 7:14	them white in the *b*

bread

Deuteronomy 8:3	not live by *b* alone
Ecclesiastes 11:1	Cast your *b* upon the
Matthew 4:4	not live by *b* alone
Matthew 6:11	this day our daily *b*
John 6:48	"I am the *b* of life
1 Corinthians 11:26	as you eat this *b*

Cc

children (child, sons)

Psalms 127:3	*c* are a heritage
Proverbs 22:6	Train up a *c* in the
Matthew 18:3	become as little *c*
Matthew 19:14	"Let the little *c*
John 1:12	the right to become *c*
Ephesians 5:8	Walk as *c* of light
Ephesians 6:1	*C*, obey your parents

church

Matthew 16:18	rock I will build My *c*
Acts 5:11	upon all the *c* and upon
Acts 8:1	arose against the *c*
Ephesians 5:23	Christ is the head of the *c*
Ephesians 5:29	the Lord does the *c*
1 Timothy 3:15	which is the *c* of

clean (cleanses)

Genesis 7:2	seven each of every *c*
Leviticus 10:10	between unclean and *c*
Psalm 24:4	He who has *c* hands and
Psalm 51:1	Create in me a *c* heart
Matthew 8:2	You can make me *c*
John 15:3	"You are already *c*
1 John 1:7	blood of Jesus *c* us from all sin

commandment (command)

Joshua 22:5	to do the *c* and the law
Proverbs 6:23	For the *c* is a lamp
Matthew 22:36	which is the greatest *c*
John 13:34	"A new *c* I give to
Romans 7:9	law, but when the *c*
Ephesians 6:2	which is the first *c*

confess

Leviticus 5:5	he shall *c* that he
Nehemiah 1:6	and *c* the sins of the
Romans 10:9	that if you *c* with
Romans 14:11	every tongue shall *c*
1 John 1:9	If we *c* our sins

counsel

Job 21:16	the *c* of the wicked is
Psalm 1:1	Who walks not in the *c*
Psalm 73:24	guide me with your *c*
Revelation 3:18	"I *c* you to buy from

covenant

Genesis 6:18	I will establish my *c*
Genesis 15:18	day the Lord made a *c*
Exodus 31:16	as a perpetual *c*
Joshua 3:3	see the ark of the *c* of
1 Chronicles 16:15	Remember His *c* always
Luke 22:20	This cup is the new *c*
Hebrews 12:24	Mediator of the new *c*

create (created, creation, creature)

Genesis 1:27	So God *c* man in His
Psalm 104:30	Spirit, they are *c*
Psalm 51:10	*C* in me a clean heart
Mark 13:19	*c* which God
2 Corinthians 5:17	Christ, he is a new *c*
Colossians 1:15	firstborn over all *c*
Colossians 1:16	Him all things were *c*

cross

Matthew 10:38	does not take his *c*
Matthew 27:32	to hear His *c*
Matthew 27:40	come down from the *c*
John 19:19	a title and put it on the *c*
1 Corinthians 1:17	lest the *c* of Christ
Galatians 6:14	glory except in the *c*
Philippians 2:8	even the death of the *c*

crown

Psalm 132:18	upon Himself His *c*
Proverbs 14:24	the *c* of the wise
Proverbs 16:31	head is a *c* of glory
John 19:5	*c* of thorns
Philippians 4:1	my joy and *c*
2 Timothy 4:8	*c* of righteousness
James 1:12	*c* of life
1 Peter 5:4	*c* of glory
Revelation 2:10	*c* of life
Revelation 3:11	no one can take your *c*
Revelation 14:14	on His head a golden *c*

Dd

delight

1 Samuel 15:22	*d* in burnt offerings and sacrifices
Psalm 1:2	But his *d* is in the
Psalm 37:4	*D* yourself also in the
Psalm 119:92	Your law had been my *d*
Romans 7:22	For I *d* in the law of

demon (evil spirit)

Matthew 9:33	when the *d* was cast out
Matthew 17:18	Jesus rebuked the *d*
Luke 7:33	you say, "He has a *d*
John 8:48	Samaritan and have a *d*
Acts 19:15	And the *e s* answered

die (dead, death)
Genesis 2:7	it you shall surely *d*
Ruth 1:17	Where you *d*, I will *d*
Psalm 118:17	I shall not *d*
Ecclesiastes 3:2	born, and a time to *d*
Matthew 26:35	"Even if I have to *d*
Matthew 28:7	He is risen from the *d*
John 6:50	eat of it and not *d*
Acts 2:24	loosed the pains of *d*
Romans 6:4	was raised from the *d*
1 Corinthians 15:22	For as in Adam all *d*
Hebrews 9:27	for men to *d* once

disciple (disciples)
Matthew 9:14	but Your *d* do not fast
Matthew 10:42	in the name of a *d*
Matthew 20:17	took the twelve *d*
Luke 14:26	he cannot be My *d*
John 8:28	but we are Moses' *d*
John 15:8	so you will be My *d*
John 21:7	*d* whom Jesus loved

doctrine (teaching)
John 7:16	"My *d* is not Mine
1 Timothy 1:10	is contrary to sound *d*
2 Timothy 3:10	followed my *d*
2 Timothy 3:16	is profitable for *d*
Titus 1:9	able, by sound *d*

Ee

earth
Genesis 1:1	created the heavens and the *e*
Exodus 9:16	declared in all the *e*
1 Chronicles 16:31	coming to judge the *e*
Job 26:7	he hangs the *e* on
Psalm 24:1	*e* is the Lord's
Matthew 5:5	shall inherit the *e*
Matthew 6:10	*e* as it is in heaven

eternal (everlasting)
Deuteronomy 33:27	*e* God is your refuge
Matthew 19:16	I do that I may have *e*
Mark 10:30	in the age to come, *e*
John 3:15	not perish but have *e*
John 6:47	believes in Me has *e*
Romans 6:23	the gift of God is *e*

evil
Genesis 2:9	of good and *e*
Genesis 3:5	knowing good and *e*
Psalm 23:4	I will fear no *e*
Proverbs 17:13	Whoever rewards *e*
Amos 5:14	Seek good and not *e*
Matthew 7:11	If you then, being *e*
Romans 12:17	Repay no one *e* for

Ff

faith
Matthew 6:30	you of little *f*
Romans 10:17	*f* come by hearing
1 Corinthians 13:13	*f*, hope and love
2 Corinthians 5:8	by *f*, not by sight
Ephesians 2:8	saved through *f*
Ephesians 6:16	the shield of *f*
Hebrews 11:6	without *f* it is impossible
James 2:5	rich in *f*
James 2:18	show me your *f*

false teachers (false prophets)
Matthew 7:15	Beware of *f p*
Luke 6:26	fathers to the *f p*
2 Peter 2:1	there will be *f t*
1 John 4:1	many *f p* have gone out

fear
Leviticus 19:14	but shall f your God
Deuteronomy 6:2	*f* the Lord your God
Psalm 23:4	of death, I will *f*
Psalm 111:10	The *f* of the Lord is
1 John 4:18	love casts out *f*

fellowship
Acts 2:42	doctrine and *f*
1 Corinthians 1:9	were called into the *f*
Galatians 2:9	the right hand of *f*
Philippians 2:1	of love, if any *f*
Philippians 3:10	and the *f* of His
1 John 1:3	also may have *f*

follow
Exodus 11:8	and all the people who *f* you
Exodus 23:2	not *f* a crowd to do evil
Deuteronomy 16:20	*f* what is altogether
Psalm 23:6	goodness and mercy shall *f* me
Matthew 4:19	"*F* me, and I will
Mark 8:34	up his cross, and *f*
John 10:5	will by no means *f*

fool

Psalm 14:1	*f* has said in his
Proverbs 10:23	is like sport to a *f*
Proverbs 12:15	*f* is right in his own
Matthew 5:22	whoever says, "You *f*

forever

Genesis 3:22	and eat, and live *f*
Psalm 136:1	His mercy endures *f*
Daniel 12:3	like the stars *f*
John 12:34	the Christ remains *f*
Philippians 4:20	and Father be glory *f*
Hebrews 7:28	has been perfected *f*
Revelation 22:5	And they shall reign *f*

forgive

2 Chronicles 7:14	*f* their sin and heal
Matthew 6:12	And *f* us our debts
Mark 2:7	Who can *f* sins but God
1 John 1:9	*f* us our sins and to

Gg

give (gift)

2 Chronicles 1:10	*g* me wisdom and
Psalm 17:1	*G* ear to my prayer
Psalm 37:4	*g* you the desires
Matthew 5:42	"*G* to him who asks
Matthew 6:11	*G* us this day
John 13:34	A new commandment I *g*
Romans 6:23	but the *g* of God is
1 Corinthians 7:7	each one has his own *g*
2 Corinthians 9:15	for His indescribable *g*

glory (glorify)

Exodus 33:18	Please, show me your *g*
1 Samuel 4:22	*g* has departed from
2 Chronicles 7:2	the *g* of the Lord had filled
Psalm 8:1	You who set Your *g*
Matthew 6:13	the power and the *g*
Luke 2:14	"*G* to God in the
Philippians 4:19	to His riches in *g*

gospel

Matthew 24:14	And this *g* of the kingdom
Matthew 26:13	wherever this *g* is preached
Mark 1:11	The beginning of the *g*
Luke 9:6	preaching the *g* and healing
Romans 1:16	not ashamed of the *g*
Ephesians 6:19	the mystery of the *g*

grace

John 1:14	full of *g* and truth
John 1:17	but *g* and truth came through Jesus
Acts 15:11	through the *g* of the Lord
Romans 3:24	freely by his *g*
Romans 5:20	where sin abounded, *g* abounded
Romans 6:14	not under law but under *g*
2 Corinthians 8:9	For you know the *g* of our Lord
2 Corinthians 12:9	My *g* is sufficient for you
Ephesians 2:8	by *g* you have been saved
1 Timothy 1:2	*g*, mercy and peace
Hebrews 4:16	the throne of *g*

Hh

heart (hearts)

Genesis 6:5	*h* was only evil
1 Samuel 16:7	Lord looks at the *h*
Psalm 111:1	with my whole *h*
Jeremiah 17:9	*h* is deceitful above
Jeremiah 24:7	I will give them a *h*
Matthew 15:19	of the *h* proceed evil
Philippians 4:7	will guard your *h*
Colossians 3:15	of God will rule in your *h*
I John 3:20	if our *h* condemns us

Heaven

Psalm 14:2	Lord looks down from *h*
Ecclesiastes 5:2	For God is in *h*
Isaiah 66:1	"*H* is my throne
Matthew 3:2	for the kingdom of *h*
Matthew 6:10	on earth as it is in *h*
Matthew 24:35	"*H* and earth will
Colossians 1:5	laid up for you in *h*
Revelation 21:1	And I saw a new *h*

Hell (grave, death)

Psalm 9:17	shall be turned into *h*
Proverbs 27:20	*H* and Destruction are
Matthew 5:22	be in danger of *h* fire
Matthew 18:9	to be cast into *h*
Luke 12:5	power to cast into *h*
James 3:6	it is set on fire by *h*

Holy Spirit

Psalm 51:11	not take Your *H S* from me
Matthew 1:20	is of the *H S*
Matthew 3:11	baptize you with the *H S*
Matthew 12:32	speaks against the *H S*
John 14:26	the Helper, the *H S*
Acts 1:8	power when the *H S* has come
Acts 13:2	the *H S* said, "Now separate
1 Corinthians 6:19	body is the temple of the *H S*

hope

Psalm 39:7	My *h* is in you
Jeremiah 14:8	O the *H* of Israel
Romans 5:5	*h* does not disappoint
1 Corinthians 13:13	And now abide faith, *h*
Colossians 1:27	Christ in you, the *h* of
Titus 1:2	the *h* of eternal life

humble (humility)

Numbers 12:3	man Moses was very *h*
2 Chronicles 7:14	will *h* themselves, and pray
Psalm 147:6	Lord lifts up the *h*
Colossians 2:18	delight in false *h*
James 4:10	*H* yourselves in the
1 Peter 5:5	and be clothed with *h*
1 Peter 5:6	*h* yourselves under the

Ii

idol (idols, idolatry)

1 Samuel 15:23	is as iniquity and *i*
Isaiah 66:3	if he blesses an *i*
1 Corinthians 8:7	thing offered to an *i*
1 Corinthians 8:19	That an *i* is anything
1 John 5:21	keep yourselves from *i*

Immanuel (Emmanuel)

Isaiah 7:14	shall call His name *I*
Isaiah 8:8	of Your land, O *I*
Matthew 1:23	*I*, which is translated

Jj

joy (joyful, rejoice)

1 Chronicles 16:33	the woods shall *r* before
Nehemiah 8:10	*j* of the Lord is your strength
Psalms 30:5	*j* comes in the morning
Luke 1:44	in my womb for *j*
Galatians 5:22	the Spirit is love, *j*
Philippians 4:4	*R* in the Lord always
Hebrews 12:2	*j* that was set before
James 1:2	count it all *j*

judge (judgment)

Deuteronomy 32:36	For the Lord will *j*
Psalm 119:66	Teach me good *j*
Isaiah 66:16	sword the Lord will *j*
Matthew 7:1	"*J* not
Hebrews 12:23	heaven, to God the *j*
1 Peter 4:17	time has come for *j*

Kk

know (knowing, knowledge)

Genesis 3:22	*k* good and evil
Exodus 6:7	*k* that I am the Lord
Job 19:25	I *k* that my Redeemer lives
Psalm 46:10	Be still and *k*
Jeremiah 31:34	saying "*K* the Lord" for
John 10:27	hear My voice, and *k*
Acts 1:7	*k* times or seasons
1 Corinthians 13:9	For we *k* in part and
2 Timothy 1:12	*k* whom I have believe
1 John 3:16	By this we *k* love

Ll

lamb

Genesis 22:7	but where is the *l*
Isaiah 53:7	He was led as a *l*
1 Peter 1:19	of Christ, as of a *l*
Revelation 5:12	"Worthy is the *L*
Revelation 12:11	by the blood of the *L*

Lamb of God

John 1:29	the *L of G* who takes
John 1:36	"Behold, the *L of G*

life (live)

Genesis 2:7	the breath of *l*
Exodus 21:23	the you shall give *l*
Job 10:12	You have granted me *l*
Psalm 119:50	word has given me *l*
Amos 5:4	"Seek Me and *l*
Matthew 6:25	not worry about your *l*
Mark 8:35	desires to save his *l*
Luke 12:15	*l* does not consist
John 1:4	*l* was the light of man
John 3:16	have everlasting *l*
John 6:35	I am the bread of *l*
John 10:15	lay down My *l* for the sheep
John 15:13	ones *l* for his friends
Galatians 2:20	*l* which I now live
Philippians 1:21	to me, to *l* is Christ
1 Timothy 6:13	of God who gives *l*
1 John 5:12	who has the Son has *l*
Revelation 21:27	the Lamb's Book of *L*
Revelation 22:19	from the Book of *L*

light

Genesis 1:3	Let there be *l*
Psalm 43:3	send out Your *l*
Psalm 119:105	a *l* to my path
Proverbs 13:9	*l* of the righteous
Isaiah 2:5	walk in the *l*
Isaiah 60:20	your everlasting *l*
Matthew 5:14	You are the *l*
Matthew 5:16	let your *l* shine
John 1:9	the true *l*
John 3:19	darkness rather than *l*
Acts 26:18	from darkness to *l*
2 Corinthians 4:6	*l* shine out of the darkness
Ephesians 5:8	as children of *l*
1 Thessalonians 5:5	the sons of *l*

love (charity, loving, lovely, loved)

Leviticus 19:18	*l* your neighbor as
Deuteronomy 6:5	*l* the Lord your God
Psalm 119:97	Oh, how I *l* Your law
Ecclesiastes 3:8	a time to *l*
Micah 6:8	do justly, to *l* mercy
John 3:16	*l* the world that
John 14:15	"If you *l* Me
Romans 13:8	to *l* one another
1 Corinthians 13:8	*L* never fails
1 Corinthians 13:13	greatest of these is *l*
Galatians 5:22	fruit of the Spirit is *l*
Philippians 4:8	whatever things are *l*
1 Timothy 6:10	For the *l* of money is
Hebrews 13:1	Let brotherly *l* continue
1 Peter 4:8	for "*l* will cover a
1 John 4:7	Beloved, let us *l*

lie (lying, falsehood)

Numbers 23:9	man, that He should *l*
Psalm 119:163	I hate and abhor *l*
Romans 1:25	truth of God for the *l*
Colossians 3:9	Do not *l* to one
Titus 1:2	God, who cannot *l*

Mm

meditate (meditation)

Joshua 1:8	but you shall *m*
Psalm 19:14	of my mouth and the *m*
Psalm 77:12	also *m* on all Your work
Psalm 119:15	*m* on Your precepts

mercy

Psalm 23:6	surely, goodness and *m*
Psalm 100:5	His *m* is everlasting
Jeremiah 6:23	and have no *m*
Micah 7:18	He delights in *m*
Matthew 5:7	they shall obtain *m*
Ephesians 2:4	rich in *m*
1 Peter 1:3	His abundant *m*

money (mammon)

Isaiah 52:3	you shall be redeemed without *m*
Matthew 25:18	and hid his lord's *m*
Luke 22:35	I sent you without *m* bag
Acts 8:20	Your *m* perish with you
1 Timothy 3:3	not greedy for *m*
1 Timothy 6:10	for the love of *m*

Nn

name

Exodus 20:7	shall not take the *n*
2 Chronicles 7:14	by My *n* will humble themselves
Psalm 8:1	excellent is Your *n*
Psalm 115:1	to Your *n* give glory
Proverbs 18:10	the *n* of the Lord is a strong tower
Proverbs 22:1	A good *n* is to be chosen
Matthew 6:9	hallowed be Your *n*
Matthew 18:20	are gathered together in my *n*
John 1:12	who believe in His *n*
John 10:3	his own sheep by *n*
Acts 4:12	there is no other *n*
Philippians 2:9	which is above every *n*
Revelation 15:4	and glorify your *n*

neighbor

Jeremiah 31:34	every man teach his *n*
Matthew 5:43	You shall love your *n*
Luke 10:29	And who is my *n*
Romans 13:9	You shall love your *n* as yourself

Oo

obey (obedience)

Deuteronomy 11:27	*o* the commandments
Mark 4:41	the wind and the sea *o* Him
Acts 5:29	*o* God rather than men
Ephesians 6:1	Children, *o* your parents
Hebrews 13:17	*O* those who rule

Pp

parable

Psalm 78:2	open my mouth in a *p*
Matthew 13:18	the *p* of the sower
Mark 4:13	Do you not understand this *p*
Luke 8:11	the *p* is this

patience (endurance, longsuffering, perseverance)

Matthew 18:26	have *p* with me
Luke 8:15	bear fruit with *p*
Romans 15:5	may the God of *p*
Galatians 5:22	joy, peace, *p*, kindness
James 1:4	let *p* have its perfect work

peace

Numbers 6:26	you, and give you *p*
Psalm 34:14	seek *p*, and pursue it
Ecclesiastes 3:8	war, and a time of *p*
Isaiah 9:6	Father, Prince of *P*
Isaiah 26:3	keep him in perfect *p*
Luke 2:14	on earth, *p* and goodwill
John 14:27	*P* I leave with you
John 16:33	in Me you may have *p*
Galatians 5:22	Spirit is love, joy, *p*
Ephesians 2:14	He Himself is our *p*

perish

Matthew 18:14	little ones should *p*
John 3:16	in Him should not *p*
Colossians 2:22	concern things which *p*
2 Peter 3:9	that any should *p*

persecute

Psalm 119:86	They *p* me wrongfully
Matthew 5:11	when they revile and *p*
John 15:20	they will also *p* you
Romans 12:14	bless those who *p* you

power

Exodus 9:16	that I may show My *p*
2 Kings 17:36	Egypt with great *p*
Zechariah 4:6	Not by might nor by *p*
Matthew 6:13	the kingdom and the *p*
Acts 1:8	you shall receive *p*
Romans 1:16	for it is the *p* of God

praise (praised)

2 Samuel 22:4	who is worthy to be *p*
1 Chronicles 29:13	And *p* Your glorious name
Psalm 9:2	I will sing *p* to Your name
Psalm 22:23	fear the Lord, *p* Him
Psalm 33:2	*P* the Lord with the harp
Psalm 66:2	Make His *p* glorious
Psalm 69:34	Let heaven and earth *p*
Psalm 150:6	everything that has breath *p*
John 12:43	more than the *p* of God
Hebrews 13:15	the sacrifice of *p*

pray

Matthew 6:6:	"But you, when you *p*
Luke 11:1	"Lord teach us to *p*
Luke 22:40	"*P* that you may not
1 Thessalonians 5:17	*p* without ceasing
1 Thessalonians 5:25	Brethren, *p* for us

pride (proud)
Psalm 40:4	does not respect the *p*
Proverbs 16:18	*P* goes before
Obadiah 3:1	The *p* of your heart has
Luke 1:51	he has scattered the *p*
1 Peter 5:5	"God resists the *p*

prayer
1 Kings 8:45	hear in heaven their *p*
Job 16:17	and my *p* is pure
Psalm 39:12	Hear my *p* O Lord
Mark 11:17	a house of *p* for all nations
Philippians 4:6	but in every thing by *p*
James 5:16	the effective, fervent *p*

pure (purify, purge)
Psalm 51:7	*P* me with hyssop
Proverbs 20:11	what he does is *p* and right
Philippians 4:8	whatever things are *p*
1 Timothy 5:22	keep yourself *p*
James 4:8	*p* your hearts

Rr

redeem (redemption)
Psalm 49:15	But God will *r* my soul
Psalm 130:8	And he shall *r* Israel
Luke 2:38	those who looked for *r*
Luke 21:28	heads, because your *r*
Romans 3:24	grace through the *r*
1 Corinthians 1:30	sanctification and *r*
Ephesians 4:30	for the day of *r*

repent
Job 42:6	I abhor myself, and *r*
Ezekiel 14:6	*R*, turn away from your idols
Matthew 3:2	*R*, for the kingdom
Mark 6:12	people should *r*

resurrection
Matthew 22:33	who say there is no *r*
John 11:25	to her, "I am the *r*
1 Corinthians 15:12	say that there is no *r*
Philippians 3:10	and the power of His *r*

riches (wealth)
1 Kings 3:13	both *r* and honor
Psalm 37:16	is better than the *r*
Proverbs 11:28	who trusts in *r* will fall
Romans 9:23	the *r* of His glory
Ephesians 1:7	the *r* of His grace
Revelation 5:12	To receive power and *r*

righteousness
Genesis 15:6	He accounted it to him for *r*
Deuteronomy 6:25	it will be *r* for us
Psalm 23:3	in the paths of *r*
Proverbs 12:28	in the way *of* r is life
Matthew 6:33	His *r*, and all these things
Galatians 2:21	if *r* comes through the law
Ephesians 6:14	the breastplate of *r*
2 Timothy 3:16	for instruction in *r*

Ss

sacrifice
Genesis 31:54	Jacob offered a *s*
1 Kings 18:38	consumed the burnt *s*
Hosea 6:6	desire mercy and not *s*
Romans 12:1	bodies a living *s*, holy,
Ephesians 5:2	offering and a *s* to God

salvation (deliverance)
Exodus 14:13	see the *s* of the Lord
2 Samuel 22:3	the horn of my *s*
Psalm 3:8	*S* belongs to the Lord
Luke 1:77	to give knowledge of *s*
Luke 19:9	Today *s* has come
Acts 4:12	is there *s* in any other
Romans 1:16	power of God to *s*
Ephesians 6:17	take the helmet of *s*
2 Timothy 2:10	*s* which is in Christ
Revelation 7:10	*S* belongs to our God

Satan
1 Chronicles 21:1	*S* stood up against
Job 1:6	before the Lord, and *S*
Matthew 4:10	"Away with you *S*
Luke 22:31	*S* has asked for you
1 Timothy 5:15	turned away after *S*
Revelation 12:9	called the Devil and *S*

serve (servant, bondservant)
Deuteronomy 6:13	your God and *s* Him
Matthew 6:24	You cannot *s* God and
Mark 10:45	but to *s*, and to give
Galatians 5:13	through love *s* one another
Ephesians 6:5	*Bs* be obedient
Colossians 2:22	*Bs* obey in all things
1 Timothy 6:1	*bs* count their masters worthy
Titus 2:9	Exhort *bs* to be obedient
Revelation 22:3	His *s* shall *s* Him

sheep (shepherd)

Genesis 4:2	Abel was a keeper of *s*
Psalm 23:1	The Lord is my *s*
Isaiah 53:7	slaughter, and as a *s*
John 10:11	"I am the good *s*
John 10:4	and I know my *s*
1 Peter 2:25	like *s* going astray

shield

Genesis 15:1	I am your *s*
2 Samuel 22:31	He is a *s* to all who trust in Him
2 Samuel 22:36	give me the *s* of your salvation
Psalm 91:4	His truth shall be your *s*
Psalm 115:9	He is their help and their *s*
Proverbs 2:7	He is a *s* to those who walk uprightly
Ephesians 6:16	above all, taking the *s* of faith

sin (sins)

Numbers 32:23	your *s* will find you out
Job 2:10	all this and Job did not *s*
Psalm 4:4	Be angry, and do not *s*
John 8:7	"He who is without *s*
John 16:8	convict the world of *s*
Romans 5:12	*s* entered the world
James 4:17	do it, to him it is *s*
1 John 1:8	say that we have no *s*
1 John 5:17	unrighteousness is *s*

soul

Deuteronomy 6:5	heart, with all your *s*
1 Samuel 1:15	my *s* before the Lord
Psalm 23:3	He restores my *s*
Matthew 10:28	able to destroy both *s*
1 Peter 2:11	which war against the *s*

Tt

tempt (temptation)

Matthew 6:13	do not lead us into *t*
Matthew 26:41	lest you enter into *t*
1 Corinthians 7:5	that Satan does not *t*
1 Corinthians 10:13	no *t* has overtaken you
James 1:13	nor does He Himself *t*

trust

Psalm 4:5	put your *t* in the Lord
Proverbs 3:5	*T* in the Lord with all your heart
Hebrews 2:13	I will put My *t* in Him

truth (true)

Psalm 51:6	Behold, you desire *t*
Psalm 96:13	the peoples with His *t*
Proverbs 23:23	Buy the *t*, and do not sell it
John 8:32	you shall know the *t*
John 14:6	"I am the way, the *t*
1 Corinthians 13:6	rejoices in the *t*
Ephesians 6:14	your waist with *t*

Uu

understanding

Job 38:36	given *u* to the heart
Proverbs 2:2	apply your heart to *u*
Proverbs 3:5	not on your own *u*
Philippians 4:7	which surpasses all *u*

unity

Psalm 133:1	to dwell together in *u*
Ephesians 4:3	to keep the *u* of the Spirit
Ephesians 4:13	we all come to the *u*

walk

Genesis 17:1	*w* before Me and be
Leviticus 26:12	I will *w* among you
Deuteronomy 10:12	to *w* in all His ways
Psalm 23:4	Yea, though I *w*
Isaiah 30:21	"This is the way, *w* in it
John 5:8	take up your bed and *w*
2 Corinthians 5:7	For we *w* by faith
1 John 1:7	if we *w* in the light

Ww

wealth

Ruth 2:1	a man of great *w*
2 Chronicles 1:11	not asked riches or *w*
Proverbs 19:4	*W* makes many friends
Revelation 18:19	became rich by her *w*

wisdom

Deuteronomy 4:6	for this is your *w*
Proverbs 3:13	is the man who finds *w*
Proverbs 9:10	is the beginning of *w*
Ecclesiastes 9:16	*W* is better than strength
Luke 2:52	Jesus increased in *w*
Romans 11:33	both of the *w* and knowledge
Colossians 4:5	Walk in *w* toward those
James 1:5	If any of you lacks *w*

witness (testimony)
Proverbs 14:5	A faithful *w* does not lie
Matthew 24:14	all the world as a *w*
John 3:11	do not receive our *w*
Acts 22:15	For you will be his *w*
Revelation 1:5	Christ, the faithful *w*

worship
Genesis 22:5	I will go yonder and *w*
Psalm 95:6	Oh come, let us *w*
Isaiah 95:6	Oh come, let us *w*
Daniel 3:12	or *w* the gold image
Matthew 2:2	and have come to *w* Him
Matthew 4:9	will fall down and *w* me
John 4:24	*w* in spirit and truth
Revelation 4:10	*w* Him who lives

Divided Kingdom

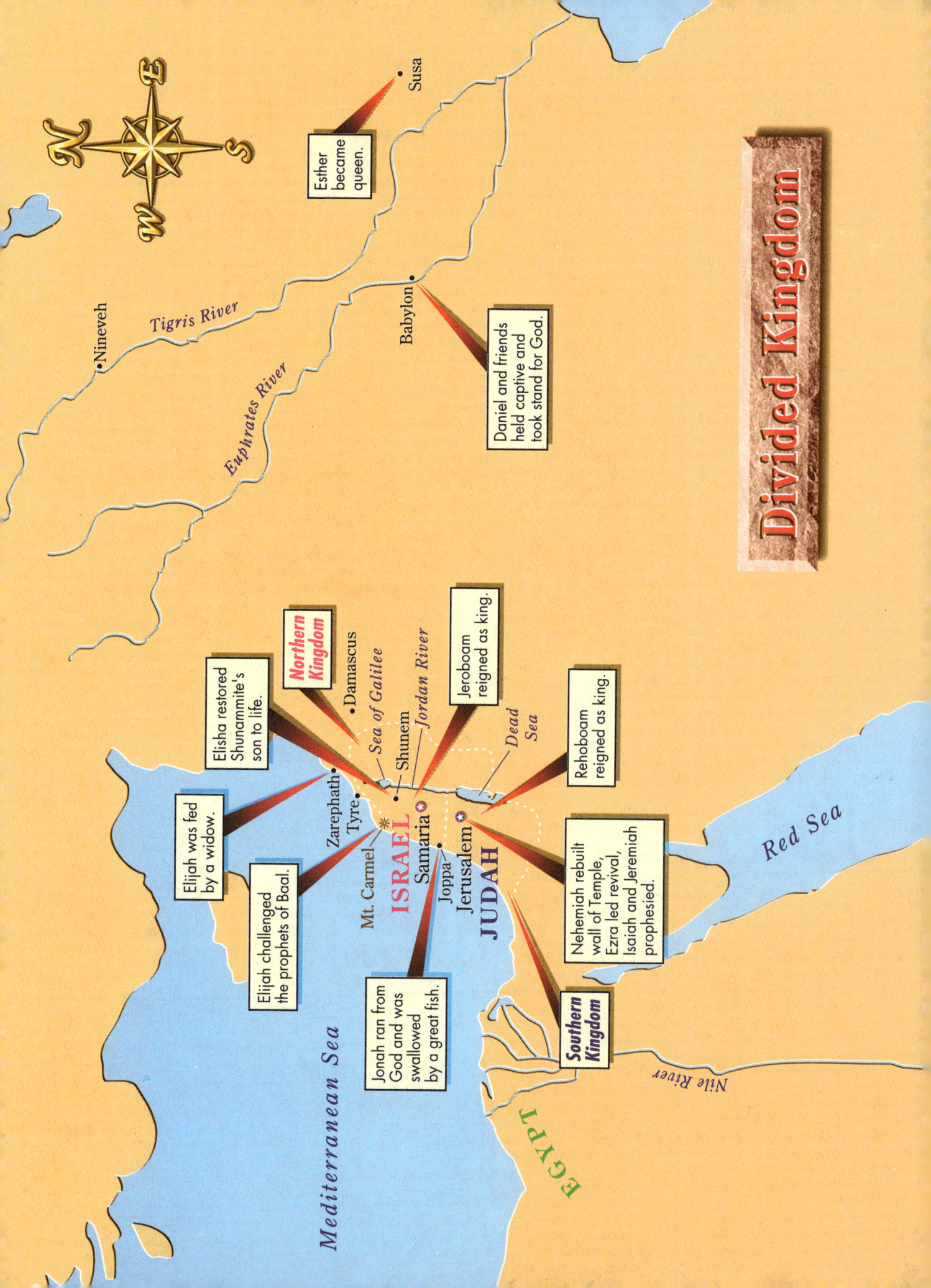

- Susa — Esther became queen.
- Babylon — Daniel and friends held captive and took stand for God.
- Nineveh
- Tigris River
- Euphrates River

Northern Kingdom
- Damascus
- Sea of Galilee
- Shunem — Elisha restored Shunammite's son to life.
- Jordan River
- Jeroboam reigned as king.
- Dead Sea
- Rehoboam reigned as king.
- Zarephath — Elijah was fed by a widow.
- Tyre
- Mt. Carmel — Elijah challenged the prophets of Baal.
- **ISRAEL** — Samaria
- Joppa — Jonah ran from God and was swallowed by a great fish.
- Jerusalem — Nehemiah rebuilt wall of Temple, Ezra led revival, Isaiah and Jeremiah prophesied.
- **JUDAH**

Southern Kingdom

- Mediterranean Sea
- Red Sea
- Nile River
- EGYPT

The Judges—United Kingdom

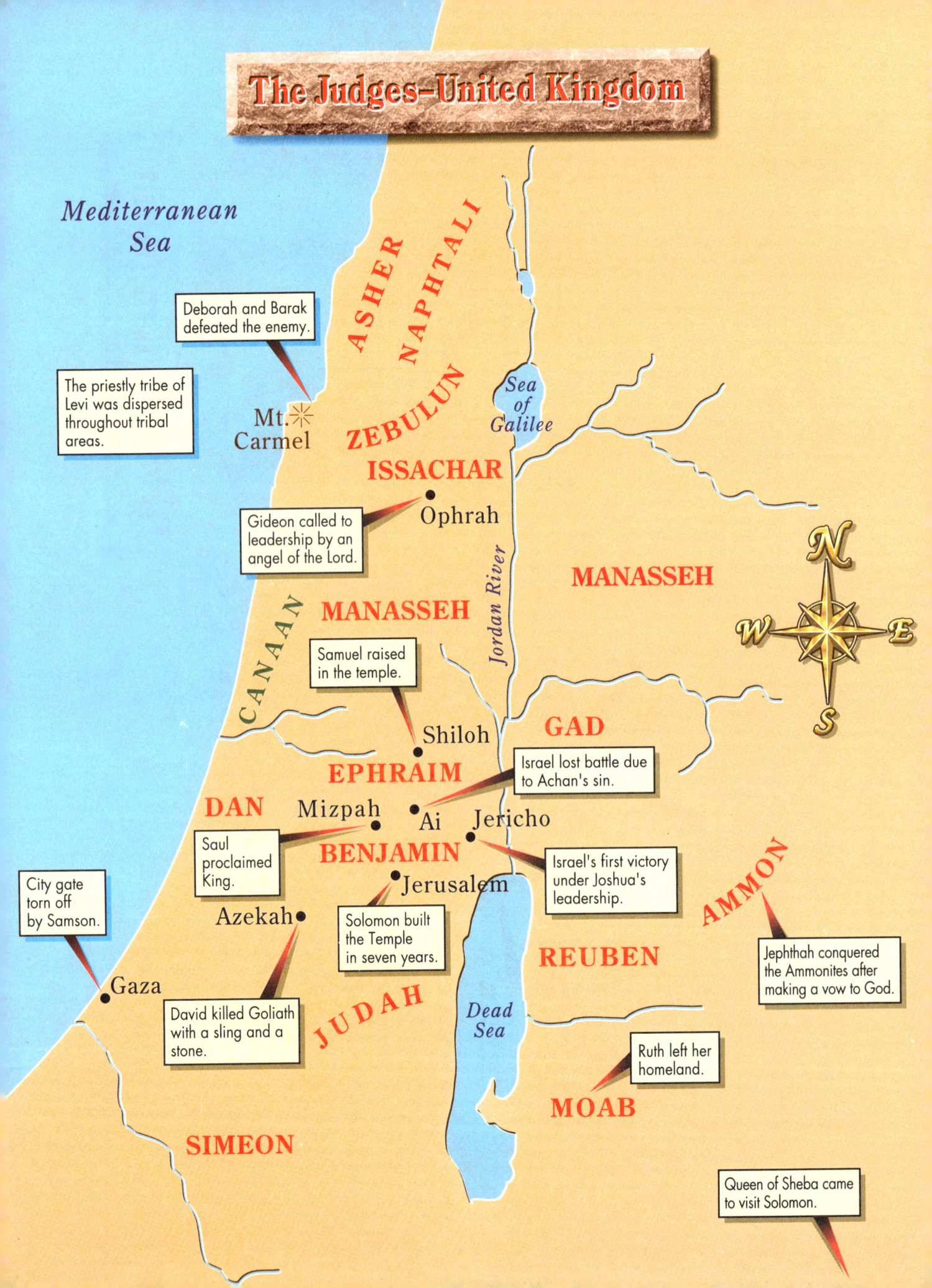

Mediterranean Sea

- Deborah and Barak defeated the enemy.
- The priestly tribe of Levi was dispersed throughout tribal areas.
- Gideon called to leadership by an angel of the Lord.
- Samuel raised in the temple.
- Israel lost battle due to Achan's sin.
- Saul proclaimed King.
- Israel's first victory under Joshua's leadership.
- Solomon built the Temple in seven years.
- City gate torn off by Samson.
- David killed Goliath with a sling and a stone.
- Jephthah conquered the Ammonites after making a vow to God.
- Ruth left her homeland.
- Queen of Sheba came to visit Solomon.

Tribes/Regions: ASHER, NAPHTALI, ZEBULUN, ISSACHAR, MANASSEH, CANAAN, GAD, EPHRAIM, DAN, BENJAMIN, REUBEN, AMMON, JUDAH, MOAB, SIMEON

Locations: Mt. Carmel, Sea of Galilee, Ophrah, Jordan River, Shiloh, Mizpah, Ai, Jericho, Jerusalem, Azekah, Gaza, Dead Sea

Divided Kingdom

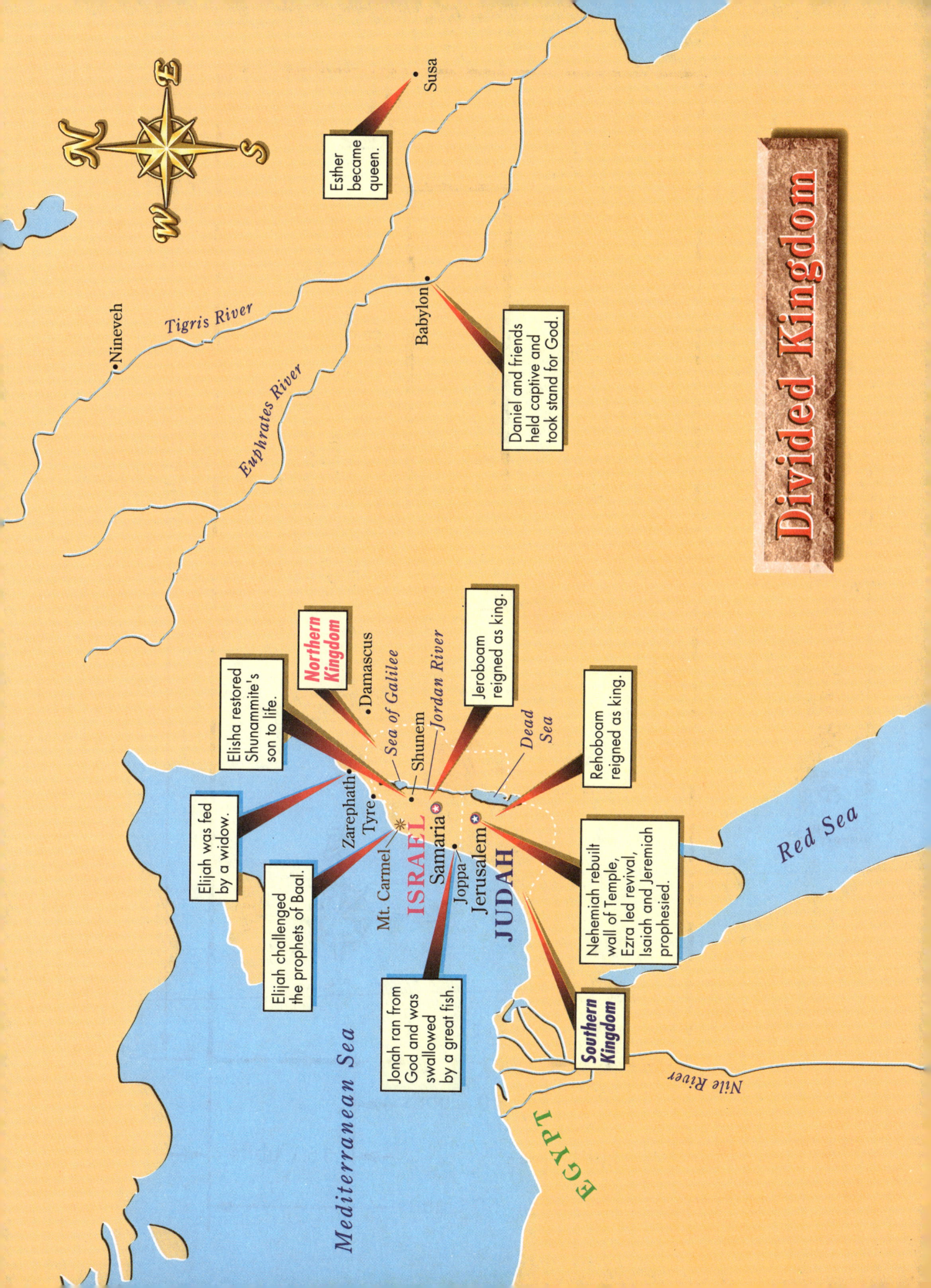

- Esther became queen. (Susa)
- Daniel and friends held captive and took stand for God. (Babylon)
- Nineveh
- Tigris River
- Euphrates River
- Elisha restored Shunammite's son to life.
- Northern Kingdom
- Damascus
- Sea of Galilee
- Shunem
- Jordan River
- Jeroboam reigned as king.
- Dead Sea
- Rehoboam reigned as king.
- Elijah was fed by a widow.
- Zarephath
- Tyre
- Mt. Carmel
- Samaria
- ISRAEL
- Elijah challenged the prophets of Baal.
- Joppa
- Jerusalem
- JUDAH
- Nehemiah rebuilt wall of Temple, Ezra led revival, Isaiah and Jeremiah prophesied.
- Jonah ran from God and was swallowed by a great fish.
- Southern Kingdom
- Mediterranean Sea
- Red Sea
- EGYPT
- Nile River

The Tabernacle

- Ark of the Covenant
- Holy of Holies
- Veil
- Incense Altar
- Showbread Table
- Golden Lampstand
- Holy Place
- Gold Columns
- Bronze Laver
- Brazen Altar
- Gate

100 Cubits
50 Cubits
20 Cubits
15 Cubits
15 Cubits

Early New Testament Jesus' Ministry

- Antioch — Church sent first missionaries.
- Sermon on the Mount
- Fed 5,000
- **GALILEE**
- Capernaum
- Bethsaida
- Sea of Galilee
- Tempted in the wilderness
- Walked on the water and calmed the storm
- Turned water into wine
- Cana
- Baptism
- Nazareth — Spent childhood
- Gadara (Gerasenes) — Healed man with demons
- Damascus — Appeared to Paul
- **SAMARIA**
- Spoke to the woman at the well
- Sychar
- Jordan River
- Crucified, Resurrected, Ascended
- Performed many miracles
- Visited the Temple
- Jericho
- Jerusalem
- Bethlehem
- Bethany — Raised Lazarus from the dead
- Birth
- Dead Sea
- **JUDEA**
- Ziph
- Taken by Joseph to Egypt
- Mediterranean Sea

Paul's Journeys
First Missionary Journey
Second Missionary Journey
Third Missionary Journey
Journey to Rome
Mediterranean Sea
MACEDONIA
THRACE
ITALY
SICILY
MALTA
ACHAIA
CRETE
RHODES
ASIA
PHRYGIA
GALATIA
BITHYNIA & PONTUS
CILICIA
CYPRUS
SYRIA
JUDEA
Rome
Three Taverns
Forum of Appius
Puteoli
Rhegium
Syracuse
Amphipolis
Apollonia
Thessalonica
Philippi
Neapolis
Berea
Troas
Assos
Pergamum
Smyrna
Mitylene
Ephesus
Laodicea
Pisidian Antioch
Iconium
Lystra
Derbe
Tarsus
Syrian Antioch
Seleucia
Corinth
Cenchrea
Athens
Miletus
Cnidus
Patara
Myra
Perga
Lasea
Fair Havens
Salamis
Paphos
Sidon
Tyre
Damascus
Ptolemais
Caesarea
Jerusalem
N
E
S
W

The World

- ASIA
- EUROPE
- AFRICA
- AUSTRALIA
- ANTARCTICA
- NORTH AMERICA
- SOUTH AMERICA

- Arctic Ocean
- Indian Ocean
- North Atlantic Ocean
- South Atlantic Ocean
- North Pacific Ocean
- South Pacific Ocean